A New Body For Life

Maggie's Method

IMPORTANT NOTICE:

THE MAGGIE DROZD METHOD IS NOT INTENDED AS A SUBSTITUTE FOR MEDICAL COUNSELING. CONSULT A PHYSICIAN BEFORE STARTING THIS OR ANY WEIGHT-LOSS PLAN, ESPECIALLY IF YOU ARE PREGNANT, BREAST-FEEDING, IF YOU TAKE MEDICATIONS, OR IF YOU ARE SEEING A PHYSICIAN FOR ANY SERIOUS HEALTH PROBLEM. THIS WEIGHT-LOSS PLAN SHOULD NOT BE FOLLOWED BY THE ELDERLY OR CHILDREN, BY PEOPLE TREATED FOR HIGH BLOOD PRESSURE OR DEPRESSION, OR WHO HAVE A HEART CONDITION, DIABETES, OR THYROID DISEASE. THIS WEIGHT-LOSS PLAN IS NOT INTENDED TO TREAT, DIAGNOSE, CARE OR PREVENT ANY DISEASE. TESTIMONIALS PUBLISHED ARE AMONG THE BEST RECEIVED. INDIVIDUAL RESULTS MAY VARY FROM ONE INDIVIDUAL TO ANOTHER AND CAN BE MORE OR LESS THAN RESULTS MENTIONED.

CAUTION

DON'T TAKE MORE THAN ONE "SPICE" CAPSULE EACH DAY. IF, BY FOLLOWING THE METHOD MAGGIE DROZD, YOU FIND THAT YOU'RE LOSING MORE THAN 10 POUNDS A WEEK FOR THE FIRST 4 WEEKS, AND MORE THAN 6 POUNDS PER WEEK FOR THE FOLLOWING WEEKS, STOP TAKING THE "SPICE" CAPSULES FOR AT LEAST 3 DAYS—THEN TAKE ONLY ONE CAPSULE EVERY OTHER DAY.

A NEW BODY FOR LIFE

Maggie's Method

- easy to use
- fantastic success
- guaranteed long-term results

Testimonials

I have received, and continue to receive, testimonials from people who have lost 20, 40, 60 pounds and more, thanks to my method.

Look at what men and women from around Europe have written to me:

"...Your method is incredibly effective. I lost 10 pounds in the first week, all while continuing to eat as much as I wanted..."
G.D. Luxembourg

"...To lose weight without counting calories, without a strict diet and without weighing foods, I thought that this was impossible. I nevertheless lost 35 pounds in this manner, only by following your method. I believe that every woman who has a difficult weight problem should try this..."
L.A. Italy

"When I saw your photos in my favorite magazine, it was a shock. I was a little bit skeptical, but I had more than 40 pounds to lose. So, I ordered your method. Today, I've already lost 37 pounds and each week, I continue to lose weight without effort. Even my husband can't believe it. I've rediscovered the pleasures of being attractive and elegant..."
C.B. Belgium

"...I lost so much weight (68 pounds in 3 months) that my doctor told me to stop. I regained the figure I had before my marriage. I really wanted to look like you in your photo because I was in the same shape as you before..."

J.F.R. Germany

"...My weight was 183 pounds on my 5'6" frame. This created within me an obstacle to my happiness. Thanks to your method, and while continuing to eat as before after two months, I now weigh no more than 145 pounds..."

B.S. England

"...When I explained to my brother how I lost 26 pounds in 3 weeks thanks to your method, he laughed. As he also had 20 pounds to lose, he also wanted to try. Today, he's no longer laughing and thanks me every day. In only one month, he lost 24 pounds and I can assure you that he doesn't pay any attention to what he eats..."

I.C. Switzerland

"...I have seen specialists. I have swallowed medicines and followed diets that made me sick. A close friend told me about your weight-loss method and I tried it because I had nothing to lose. In two months, I lost 42 pounds and since then I haven't regained anything..."

M.D. Germany

"...I lost 29 pounds in 5 weeks and I don't gain back my extra weight anymore. A new life is beginning for me..."

M.A. Switzerland

You can also see the photos sent to me by three women, from Hungary and from Poland. You have to admit that they're impressive (one lost 44 pounds, the others 58 and 59 pounds, and the fourth 95 pounds).

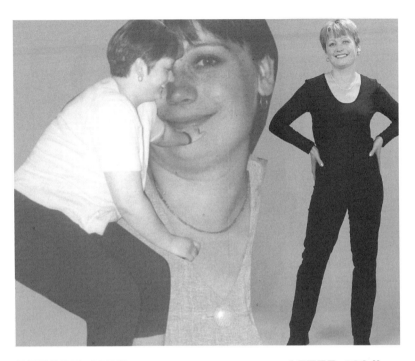

BEFORE: 185 lbs.   AFTER:126 lbs.

Lilla Porebska, Poland: *"I lost 59 pounds and people ask me how I did it."*

"Just like you, I had tried different diets and products, without results. When I read your article in the Polish press, I was skeptical. Before starting, I weighed 185 pounds. Now, I've already lost 59 pounds... I was so glad to be able to lose weight without being hungry. I thank you, because I am very happy."

BEFORE: 222 lbs.

Katarzyna G., Gostynin

"I've waited 6 months before writing to you, just to be sure that I didn't gain back the 95 pounds I lost...."

"In the month of March, 2000, I received the Maggie Drozd weight-loss plan. I then weighed 222 pounds (I'm 5'5" tall). For as long as I can remember, I've always been big. From the age of 12, I started gaining from year to year. I had followed several diets, but each time that I lost between 20 to 30 pounds, I gained them back quickly. It was horrible: I was always hungry, I felt faint, I was always counting calories. I was

very self conscious and I suffered a lot, psychologically.

Then, I discovered the
Maggie Drozd weight-
loss plan one day while
reading a newspaper. I
was skeptical, but I de-
cided to try it anyway...

I lost a total of 95
pounds and now I
weigh 127 pounds. I've
waited 6 months before
writing to you, because I
wanted to be sure that
there was no 'yo-yo' effect.

Today, I know that
there is no such effect,
because my weight has
remained steady...

I want to thank Maggie
Drozd because my life
has changed thanks
to her. Her weight-loss
plan is really not dif-
ficult to follow and it's
because of her that I
am now so happy."

AFTER:
127 lbs.

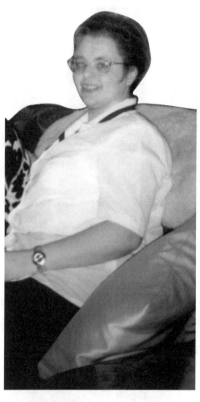 

BEFORE   AFTER

Igaz Ildiko, Hungary: *"I lost 44 pounds to become a stewardess."*

"I am sending you these pictures because now I can dare to show myself to the world with pride. You can see the difference—I've lost 44 pounds. Since I've lost my excess weight, I am working as a stewardess, I am very happy, and I feel very pretty."

BEFORE: 211 lbs.   **AFTER: 153 lbs.**

Lidia Piorecka, Poland: *"I still can't believe it... I went from 211 to 153 pounds very quickly."*

"I am writing to inform you of the results that I obtained very quickly. I decided to lose weight the day when my weight reached 211 pounds. Thanks to your method, today I weigh 153 pounds and I can prove it. When I compare an older photo with the most recent pictures of me, I have the impression that they're of two different people. I can't believe it myself..."

BEFORE: At 192 pounds, I had become obese, and unrecognizable because I was deformed by my excess weight.

Maggie Drozd has played in 2 award-winning films at the Cannes film festival. More than 8 million viewers can watch her each day on television. Already, hundreds of thousands of people have tried, with success, the method for losing weight without dieting that is revealed to you in this book.

Looking at these before/after photos of Maggie Drozd, many people have difficulty believing that it is really the same person in each photo, so great is the change after having lost her excess weight.

"I, Francois Frank, Notary, certify that the photographs are original prints which have been entrusted to me and which remain on deposit in my office, this permits me to conclude that the photographs are of the same person, and have not been falsified. Signed in the Year 2001, on the 8th day of October, at 2:00 PM."

AFTER: At 126 pounds, I was called the Sexiest Woman of the Evening at a fashion show put on by France's top fashion designer.

Preface

Yes, I lost 66 pounds without following a diet and I was able to get back the figure of my 20s thanks to an astonishing encounter with a Swiss nutritionist.

All the European television viewers can attest that I lost 66 pounds in a few months. When I appear in the European newspapers with the largest circulations, it isn't just because I'm a star of many television series, but also because of my extraordinary weight loss. Certain journalists do not hesitate to write "Maggie Drozd looks younger by ... 66 pounds!!"

Journalists wanted to know my secret, and they took advantage of my tour through England to make an appointment for an interview in a famous London restaurant. The revelations that you are going to discover in this book are going to surprise you, but also permit you to finally lose those extra pounds that you haven't successfully lost to this day.

Extracts from an exclusive interview with Elisabeth Palmer:

Question: My dear Maggie, when I see you looking so slim, young and ravishing, I have trouble believing that you ever looked as you did in the photos before your weight loss. Not only have you lost so much weight, but you also look 20 years younger.

Answer: Elisabeth, thank you for the compliment, but everything is true and all the world could see that in my films and TV shows I weighed an extra 66 pounds. I cannot tell you where and when, but you will soon see me on television again just as you see me today, 66 pounds lighter. Now I'm going to tell you the full story, which began about 2 years ago.

In those days, I weighed 192 pounds and, as you can see in the photos, I was really obese and unrecognizable, so greatly were my figure and face distorted by the weight. On a professional level, this began to cause problems for me. I was getting fewer and fewer interesting roles. And one day, I was surprised to find myself called "the huge one." I was terribly upset.

That same night, I was crying so much that I decided to talk to my husband about what happened. His response helped reinforce my decision I had to lose weight quickly, once and for all.

Question: Had you tried to lose weight before?

Answer: You know, I didn't wait until I reached 192 pounds (I'm 5'6" tall) before trying to lose weight. I tried everything. I saw doctors. I followed diets. I tried crash treatments. I probably tried every miracle method that appeared since the early 90s. I spent a lot of money for nothing. When I lost 5 pounds, and felt like I was starving, I regained 10 pounds in a few days. With a very well-known treatment, that was the worst; I lost 22 pounds in 2 months and then I regained exactly 37 in one month. Result: 15 more pounds!

Question: We read in all the newspapers with the largest circulations – Polish, Russian, Italian, German, British, Swiss, and I forget how many other countries – that you lost 66 pounds while eating what you wanted and as much as you were used to eating. I must admit that I have trouble believing this. Can you tell me if this is really what you did?

Answer: Yes, it's all true. I discovered my secret a little over

"I lost 66 pounds while continuing to eat all that I wanted, and everything that I liked."

two years ago, when I was flirting with the 200-pound mark. I was skiing in Switzerland. With my weight, I was having trouble skiing and I was terribly bored and frustrated.

One day when I was reading on a sunny terrace at the hotel, someone approached me and asked if I was Polish (I was reading a Polish magazine). Though a Swiss citizen, she was Polish herself and she was happy to speak Polish. She worked as a nutritionist in a well-known health spa. We quickly became friends, and I naturally started to tell her about my weight problems.

After a few questions, she reassured me and told me that, in the spa where she was working, they helped the most famous celebrities lose weight with a revolutionary method. She had even participated in its development. Each day she described, little by little, the main principles of this new method that didn't resemble anything that I had tried before.

Question: *What can you tell us about this secret?*

Answer: You know, despite everything, I was skeptical. When you've tried so many weight-loss methods, you start believing that nothing works. But I was quickly forced to admit that this method worked. I rapidly lost 35 pounds in only 5 weeks. During the following 2 months, I lost another 31 pounds, for a total of 66 pounds.

Question: *But you had lost some weight with the other methods...*

Answer: That's true, but there are 3 new and different aspects to this method:

1. It's been almost 2 years since I've lost the weight, and I have not regained a single ounce.

2. I am continuing to lose weight. I'm not paying close attention (because I don't weigh myself anymore), but I believe that I've lost another 4 or 5 pounds.

3. During the time when I was losing most of the weight, I continued to eat in restaurants like today. I ate pasta, cakes and even chocolate (things that normally make me gain weight).

Question: *How can we learn more about this secret?*

Answer: With the agreement of my nutritionist friend, who told me all about it, I've explained the method in a special report, about which I can be a bit more precise:

1. This has nothing to do with a diet or exercise (I'm not very athletic). You can do it on your own, at home. You can even do it at restaurants or while on vacation.

2. Because I'm fond of good food, the most important thing is that I'm able to eat what I want and not deprive myself. With this method, you can eat everything, and as much as you want.

3. This method is pleasant, natural, and excellent for your health. It permits you to lose 6 to 10 pounds each week for the first few weeks and 4 to 6 pounds per week afterwards – even if you eat pasta, rice, cakes, buttery foods, sugary foods, or even fatty meats. There are no restrictions.

Question: I've heard that this method contains "spices". Is it thanks to the "spices" that you lose weight so quickly?

Answer: The "spices", in addition to the method, accelerate the weight-loss effect. These "spices", which are 100% natural and are therefore totally safe, stimulate the digestion and help to burn excess fat. This specific combination of "spices" is truly revolutionary and is furnished with the method in easy-to-swallow, flavorless capsules. All you have to do is take one of these capsules with your main meal.

Question: To lose weight, people should use your method and, if they want to lose weight faster, they simply have to take one of these "spice" capsules with their main meal, correct?

Answer: Yes, the "spices", when combined with the method, accelerate the weight loss. And even if you don't like spices, let me reassure you that these are very mild and agreeable "spices" that will only help you lose weight faster. What's more, they're hermetically sealed in easy-to-swallow capsules, and have no taste themselves.

Question: You say that you can eat anything and not deprive yourself. But isn't it impossible to lose weight while eating whatever you want?

Answer: No, it's not impossible anymore. My nutritionist friend explained to me why we cannot efficiently lose weight by depriving ourselves (the yo-yo effect). She told me this: "Nine people out of ten who follow a diet based on food-deprivation actually lose weight. But once they start eating normally again, they regain the weight. This is because the human metabolism is made a certain way. When you are deprived of your habitual foods, it compensates automatically." She then explained that the main reason why I lost 66 pounds and why I've never regained them is because I continued to eat what I wanted, and as much as I wanted.

Question: How many pounds can we lose in a week?

Answer: The weight-loss rate varies from person to person. With the method associated with the "spice" capsules, you can lose up to 12 pounds in the first week. Myself, I lost 11 pounds in the first week, and 6 pounds each week for the next four weeks. After, I continued to regularly lose 4 pounds a week.

Question: Can you tell me how it feels to regain your slim figure?

Answer: Believe me, this surpasses everything that I could imagine. With my new figure, I relaunched my career and you will see me in quite a few new shows a little bit everywhere, on television, and in movie theaters. Numerous producers have called me. My husband looks at me as if I were a new woman. A few months ago, at a fashion show put on by France's top fashion designer, I was voted the Sexiest Woman of the Evening. Even if this causes a few jealousies, I have to admit that it's very pleasant.

Question: What would you say to our readers who have weight problems, and who have trouble getting rid of their extra weight?

Answer: I'd simply say this: You may have tried everything— diets, medications, maybe even methods that were risky for your health, or exercises that exhausted you. I've tried everything as well. Truly everything. And it's all come to nothing. The only thing that worked for me is the secret that my Swiss nutritionist friend shared with me. This secret, which is used in a renowned health spa, was revealed to only a few people, of whom I am lucky to be one.

In only one year, my method has helped hundreds of thousands of people in Europe. It is widely distributed in at least twelve countries in Europe, such as Poland, Russia, Hungary, Germany, Italy, Switzerland, England, etc., and will soon be available in other countries as well.

Thank you, Maggie Drozd, for this interview. I'll let my readers know that, during this meal, you drank wine, and ate everything: an appetizer, an entree and a dessert.

London, the 17th of October, 2001.

Introduction

"I'm an actress! My dream has come true. I'm an actress - at least that's what it says on my diploma. Today, 6 June, I got my MA in dramatic arts, so now I'm an actress! What now? So many other talented actors and actresses graduated from the Academy at the same time as I did. Every one of us has just one dream - to act, to act, and to keep on acting. Will we be successful? Will I be successful? What will the future bring us? I really shouldn't worry. For the last two years I've been on the stage, and not a bad one either - The Little Theatre (Teatr Maly). The best directors and actors work there. Every performance is an event. And I, a young, skinny ex-student and now a newly qualified actress, am part of this "great troupe".

These were some of the thoughts that raced through Maggie Drozd's head on that June day in 1980 when she receive her longed-for diploma from the State Academy of Dramatic Arts (PWST) in Warsaw. A day on which the dreams of a young girl, who always knew she wanted to be an actress, came true. Maggie was brought up with this goal in mind, in a wonderful family atmosphere. Her parents took her to the National Philharmonia to "Auntie Jadzia's Concerts", to the opera and to the theatre to see the best performances.

Maggie was fascinated. She did not dream about the socialist slogans that were popular at that time, but only of being on the

21

stage herself. She listened to Paul Anka, Tom Jones, Led Zeppelin, as well as rock stars and groups from her own country. Maggie's passions for the thespian and culinary arts grew, nourished by the atmosphere at home - the gatherings of her numerous relations, the singing, the dancing and the cordon bleu cookery of her parents. Her father was the director of an investment bank and her mother, a key figure at the PeKaO SA Bank. Which career should Maggie choose? Preferably a combination of everything. She created her own culinary "works" and then consumed them without a thought. After all, she had graduated as a slim young girl. At this time she was singing in a well-known group called "Amfonia" and was crowned with success at various song festivals. As well as these artistic and acting activities she passed her A-levels almost incidentally and was suddenly confronted with the decision of what to do with the rest of her life. It would probably be best to throw herself right into the action, she thought, just like she usually did.

So Maggie applied for training at several different establishments - as a stewardess, to archaeological and Romanic faculties of universities and to the Academy of Dramatic Arts. What would come of it? She would let Fate decide.

In the event, Fate saved Maggie from a lot of decision-making by deciding immediately that she should become an actress - the entrance exams for the Academy of Dramatic Arts were held earlier than the entrance exams for the other training establishments. She prepared excerpts from several well-known works, including the Decameron, Lilla Weneda and Konopielka. When asked how many balconies there were at the Polski Theater she replied, "Two, of course". Then, despite her low register, she sang a soprano piece, "Hark how the thrushes sing". It was not luck but talent that led the horribly demanding committee to award her the highest marks of all the candidates accepted by the

Academy. Among her fellow students were Maria Pakulnis, Dorota Kwiatkowska, Agnieszka Kotulanka, Agnieskzka Fatyga, Michalem Bajorem, Krzysztof Tyncem and Krzysztof Luft, all of whom were to become very famous in her native Poland.

The troupe embarked on a series of foreign tours, playing "Madame Tussaud's Waxworks" under the directorship of Tadeusz Lomnicki, rector of the Warsaw Academy of Dramatic Arts. Mail played the role of Joan of Arc. The troupe played in Holland, Finland, the Soviet Union, and was invited to a reception in the Swedish King's palace. This was followed by a stay of several months at an exotic theatrical academy in India.

There was no lack of interesting and humorous experiences during these trips, and one of them had to do with eating. In Finland, at a reception given by the Mayor of Helsinki, Maggie ate absolutely nothing, because she had no idea what she should eat and what she should eat it with. When she arrived back at her hotel, ravenous as a wolf, she went to the dining room to finally satisfy her hunger. But when she ordered a delicious, sumptuous meal using her VIP card, the mayor turned up and whisked her off to an exclusive disco in the middle of town, where Diana Ross was appearing. And there they had only bread sticks and salted almonds to eat! The next morning, in the plane, she was presented with a bouquet of roses by way of an apology for spoiling her dinner.

Maggie's years as a student went by very fast. It was a wonderful, light-hearted time. The unforgettable Andrzej Szczepkowski wished her a career as terrific as her results as a student had been. The adventure of a life in the theatre began during her third year at the Academy, when she played the part of Era in Adam Hanuszkiewiczs' production of Dziady at the Little Theatre. After finishing her studies Maggie was taken on by the New Theatre (Teatr Nowy) in Warsaw, where she was thrown in at the deep end on the very first day of the new season. One of the principal actresses had decided to stay in the West, and Maggie was suddenly asked to take over her part. She spent fourteen wonderful years at the New Theatre, which became her home from home. She made guest appearances at the Modern Theatre (Teatr Wspolczesny) and 1980 onwards she and her colleagues gave concerts in churches.

All theatre wardrobes are hotbeds of rumours. Every-body knows everything and more about everybody else - who's sleeping with whom, who shouldn't sleep with whom, who is getting uglier, who is getting older, who has gained weight and how much. Years went by and Maggie remained as slim as ever. She ate everything she wanted, in as much quantity as she wanted, while those around her talked about losing weight and miracle diets and how hard it was to get rid of that sudden accumulation of extra kilos and the suddenly visible spare tyres. Everybody wanted to live up to the ideal of the slim, long legged models that were always in the papers. Suddenly Maggie succumbed to the general psychosis and became scared by the prospect of gaining weight. She decided that now might be a good time to try to get her uncontrollable appetite under control by going on a diet.

First she tried the Oriental Diet. Then she tried a healthy and scientifically approved diet developed for American Astronauts. There was even a fortnight's hard grind during which she chewed on nothing but boiled wheat. People round about were feasting while Maggie went around like a martyr with a bowl of cooked seeds in her hand.

The only problem was, instead of losing weight; Maggie was astonished to find that she was gaining it at the rate of one or two kilos more each month. She couldn't understand why, parti-cularly when she was permanently dieting! She still gave sumptuous dinner parties in her flat in Warsaw's Ursynów district, but she never tried the delicious meals she had prepared because she didn't want to put on any more weight.

At that stage, Maggie didn't have a huge complex about her weight, although it did bother her slightly that suddenly all the film roles she was being offered were tubby housewives and in the theatre she only ever seemed to be cast in character parts. Of course, she missed wearing all her old favourite clothes, but she wasn't worried enough to stop sunbathing topless on the crowded beaches of the Côte d'Azur, in sunny Spain and Greece and even Africa.

Sometimes she did think that fate was a little unjust. "I don't eat sweet things, I only eat soup with my eyes, and can only dream of knuckles of pork or pasta." But it wasn't until she was asked to play the part of King Jan III Sobieski instead of Ubica in "King Ubu" that she really began to get concerned. The acting roles were still coming in, she was working often enough, but she didn't like the fact that casting directors were only thinking of her in terms of overweight "auntie" parts. Despite months of strict dieting and deprivation, her weight had now reached at an all-time high of 87 kilos. She was still a young woman, but clearly, no one was going to entrust her with the role of a young lady.

Every year, Maggie and her husband would have a skiing holiday together. One particular year, they decided to go to Switzerland. It was a really super holiday. Is there anything more lovely than snow-covered Alpine slopes in the sunshine? She had always loved sports. She played tennis, swam, rode a bike and skied. But this year, she bagan to worry… however would she manage the pistes with so much weight? Skiing downhill was no problem, but what on earth would happen if she fell? How would she be able to get up again?

When she looks back on that fateful moment now, Maggie shudders with horror. For as it turned out, she did indeed fall. Fortunately, it was not a serious fall in that she didn't break any bones or sustain any damage that would have prevented her from getting up and carrying on. But the damage to her pride was immense when she found that she couldn't get back up on her feet. When she did manage to stand, her (admittedly not inconsiderable) weight pulled her back down again like a hefty sack of potatoes. The other skiers gathered round her. Everyone tried to help her and give her advice; how to place the skis, where to put the pole in, etc., but it was all in vain. Every attempt just ended with a thud! Finally, Maggie's husband removed her skis and she was able to get up in the normal way... but, not surprisingly, Maggie had lost her desire for skiing.

She spent the next few days not on skis but on a sun lounger on the terrace where she browned her voluptuous figure in the sun.

"Are you Polish?" The unexpected question interrupted Maggie's reading. She looked up from her book and saw a well-dressed woman who was speaking to her in Polish laced with a strong foreign accent.

"Yes," Maggie replied, puzzled.

"I have seen you here for the last few days, but only when I saw you reading a Polish book did I decide to talk to you. Because I am of Polish descent." The woman said.

And so it was that Maggie and Ann-Marie struck up an acquaintance that soon became a warm friendship. Ann-Marie talked about her family and her work. Maggie talked about herself, her parts in films and plays and her plans for the future. After some time had passed, Maggie finally admitted to Ann-

Marie why she had stopped skiing and was sunbathing on the terrace.

"Would you like to lose weight?" Ann-Marie asked her.

"I think so," said Maggie. "Although I haven't got any weight-related complexes about myself in general, I am rather fed up with looking like my own aunt and having to play parts like that. Women the same age as me play young, attractive women, whereas I... Well I'd rather not talk about it. I've tried everything to lose weight, but nothing has worked. Even when I did lose a little bit of weight I quickly put it back on again.

That's when Ann-Marie told Maggie about work in a well known Swiss Clinic that specialized in the latest health and beauty treatments.

Ann-Marie explained to Maggie what a healthy diet consisted of and how overweight people were being helped in the Swiss centre where she worked. She also told Maggie in great detail how the human body worked:

"The human body, which evolved thousands of years ago, simply does not recognise the expression 'slimming diet'. To the body, any restriction - i.e., hunger - spells mortal danger. It automatically goes into defence mode to protect itself against famine. What happens then is that your body's metabolism slows down and restricts the amount of fatty tissue it burns up for fuel. All it is concerned with is building up reserves and conserving as much fat as it can to see it through the forthcoming famine. The problem is, your metabolism adjusts itself to a slower rate, and **stays at that level, even when the starvation period has ended**. That's when, even if you lose several kilos, every kilo is likely to return when your diet is over... and very often even more... This explains the yo-yo effect."

Maggie listened to Ann-Marie's words with great interest, but she did not want to believe it, even though she know that she had only started to gain weight when she had embarked on her first diet. All the same, there was a lot of logic in what Ann-Marie had said. Given that she worked at a renowned clinic, Maggie had to concede that Ann-Marie (whose figure was fabulous) was the weight-loss expert.

All too soon, Maggie's stay in the Alps came to an end and she had to go back to Poland to work. However, the new friends determined to stay in contact and Maggie promised to give Ann-Marie's advice some serious thought. But after she got back from her holiday Maggie was swamped with work. Soon she was back to her old habits - eating as little as possible, skipping meals, trying every new diet her colleagues talked about. Everything went back to "normal", including her weight. Eighty-seven kilos!

Life begins at 40!

On her 40th birthday Maggie was given a cake that was the same shape and size as her breasts... which bore the message: Life should be good to everyone ... That was when Maggie remembered what Ann-Marie had told her. She had received a birthday card from her friend which, along with Ann-Marie's good wishes, included the question: when was Maggie finally going to take Ann-Marie's message to her, that in order to lose weight, she had to **eat**. Maggie took a long critical look at herself, and then she looked at her cake and decided that she was going to take her friend's advice - starting right now. So she started on her delicious, voluptuous birthday cake. Soon she was redis-covering the delights of dining at some of her old favourite gourmet restaurants, the luxury of indulging in her beloved marzipan and carrot cakes, and once again adding pasta to her shopping list. Maggie was learning to love food again and she really could not understand how she had managed without such things for so long!

Several weeks went by in this happy state. Maggie could not really believe that eating so well could do anything but add weight to her figure, so one morning she stepped on the scales to see just how much she had gained. The pointer did indeed move quite dramatically from its usual resting-place, but not in the direction she expected it to - it actually showed a whole five kilos less! Were the scales out of order, or was Ann-Marie perhaps right? Certainly her clothes did feel a little looser on her.

Maggie carried on with her new eating regime and the next time she stepped on the scales she could hardly believe her eyes - she had lost 10 kilos. The weight just kept dropping off, while Maggie continued to enjoy her food. After losing 30 kilos some of her acquaintances did not recognise her and often walked right on by. Film Directors looked at her as if she was a stranger, and friends joked that her beloved husband must be starving her. Some even looked her up and down to see if they could see scars from plastic surgery. Her agent exclaimed: "What do you look like?" She replied, "I can look even better, just wait and see."

When you see the young slim female doctor in Jerzy Stuhr's film "A Week in the Life of a man", you can hardly believe it's the same actress who played the frumpy judge in "Love Stories" or the fat secretary in "Killer". Maggie regained the figure she had enjoyed as a youngster and got just as active again, too. She cycles, roller skates, swims, plays tennis and has even taken to the slopes skiing again, minus the fear of someone having to prop her up should she fall. Colleagues who have seen her eating normally and not sticking to any faddy diet are suspicious that there must be something sinister behind such an incredible weight loss.

What is behind Maggie's great success is a simple rule learnt from her dear friend Ann-Marie: **to lose weight you should feed yourself quite normally, eat often and regularly, and not go without meals.** Ann-Marie taught her so much about healthy eating, using herbs and spices, ensuring a rich intake of vitamins, minerals and trace elements, eating plenty of fruit and vegetables, food combining and all about the magical properties of green tea.

Read on to find out all about Maggie's successful slimming regime...

Never deny yourself food!

Never, ever again will I forbid myself food! I tried all those cranky diets and the result was weight gain and feeling unhealthy and miserable. Now I enjoy food and enjoy my life.

We live in a society in which we are always being told what to eat and what not to eat (more of the latter) and we are often made to feel guilty because we consume the 'wrong' food. Arguments about so-called bad nutrition are increasing and I have even heard the statement that "eating is like gradually dying". Forever being told that so many things are bad for us makes us feel stressed and we can hardly avoid it if we read papers and magazines or listen to the TV or radio. Well, I decided to rebel against it, because I believe that eating means living.

The 'Technical' Bit!

Like machines, which need a supply of energy in order to work (fuel, coal, electricity etc), the human body also needs different materials to produce energy and heat - to stay alive. The following may seem a little technical, but don't be put off, it is actually quite simple and just helps to illustrate one main point - *we need to eat and drink plenty to live healthily.*

An average, reasonably active healthy man or woman should every day:

- eat 1.5 to 1.75 kg of food of various kinds
- drink 2 litres of water
- take about 23,000 breaths
- breath in 10,000 to 12,000 litres of air (2,400 litres of oxygen)
- produce 1 to 2 litres of saliva
- lose 1 to 2 litres of sweat.

During the course of one day this same man or woman should excrete:

- 2.5 litres of water (2500 gr.),
- 100 gr. harmful gas,
- 20 gr. urea
- 25 gr. mineral salts

I.e. a total of about 3,560 gr. (3.65 kg.) metabolic waste.

So you see we are a wonderful and complicated machine which, like all other machines, needs fuel. We burn up the fuel to keep going, expel the waste - then need re-filling! Our major fuel is food, which enables our bodies to function and keeps our organs in a healthy state.

Essential Nutrients

As I learnt from Anne-Marie all about the many and varied nutrients and the roles they play in our body, I did wonder, with there being so very many of them, whether we could actually manage without a few. My research soon showed me that no, we cannot skimp on them if we desire optimum health. Each and every nutrient is useful, even essential!

Proteins, for example, are both a building material and a source of energy. Muscles, bones, skin, glands, hormones, enzymes and even antibodies consist of proteins and they are also used for the formation, repair and maintenance of genes. Proteins are composed mainly of amino acids - something the body cannot produce for itself - and a complete lack of amino acids means death. Protein derived from animals (meat, fish, eggs and dairy produce) contains a more complete set of amino acids than vegetable proteins (barley, legumes, etc.), but both are essential for life.

Fats have had a bad press for a long time now - with low fat diets all the rage for the health and figure conscious. However, fat is actually very important for the human body, indeed it would seem to be indispensable. Fat is indeed full of calories (about 9.3 kcal per gram), but calories or not you cannot do without it - it provides the energy for the proper functioning of the muscles, it also aids the synthesis of several hormones (especially sex hormones), and many vitamins are only soluble in fat, so without it you may become vitamin deficient.

And who hasn't heard of a low-carbohydrate diet? Well one thing such a diet will do is make you lose energy. Carbohydrates ensure that muscles work properly. There are two types: easily assimilated, water-soluble saccharides (like in white sugar, fruit, honey and milk) which reach the blood after a few minutes and types like dextrin (contained in barley products, rice, potatoes and legumes), which is characterised by its lengthy assimilation process.

I am not going to go into detail here about the many vitamins which are essential and are present in almost everything, especially fresh products and those eaten raw, because there are many books available should you wish to find out more. The same goes for mineral salts and trace elements such as calcium, phosphorous, potassium and sodium. For now it is enough for you to know that they are all simply indispensable for a healthy life.

Even if you do not quite understand the rules of healthy nutrition, what is really important for you to understand is the fact that you have got to eat to stay alive. It is that simple...

Eating is ESSENTIAL!

You don't have to be fat ...

Today my own personal 'fat' nightmare has ended. The super-fluous fat which for years hindered my every movement, which made me pant at even the slightest exertion, and which was so damaging to my career and my self-esteem has finally gone - for good.

Over the years I have tried time and time again to regain my slim figure by going on lots of well-known low-fat, low-carbohydrate, low-sugar, 'low-everything' diets. On most of these diets I would actually lose a bit of weight to start with, but then as soon as I started to eat "normally", I would put it all back on again after a few days.

My life was becoming unbearable. I had two sets of clothing, one to use when the diets were working and I was a bit slimmer, the other for the overweight periods. Every time the 'slimmer' dresses and skirts got too small for me I would panic and resolve to lose weight yet again - it was so stressful. Although I have always really loved my food, I condemned myself to punishing starvation diets - largely to please my agent and my audiences!

These extreme weight fluctuations were harming my health - I could feel it. Too much fatty tissue and the stress to which all that are in the public eye are subjected were having a negative influence on my heart. This was no longer just about how I looked, it was about my health and well being, too.

It is wonderful that today, following my own experience, I can tell you that without a doubt it is possible to lose weight quickly and healthily. You don't have to suffer from stomach cramps caused by hunger, or direct covetous looks in the direction of your neighbour's dinner plate. And what is most important of all - you can do it *without putting your health at risk*. Being overweight can have many causes, but I hope that everyone who wants to will find the solution to their problems in this book.

I am living proof. If you decide to follow my advice you will be delighted to see that you can also make a positive change in your appearance - and in your well being - without too much effort.

My weight fluctuations have been 'news' for some time now, it is really par for the course if you are in the public eye! So, you have probably seen the reports and pictures in the press, for once sharing some good news - that I have recently lost a whole lot of weight, a staggering 30 kilos. Of course everyone wants to know 'how?' Many have asked me if I've been on a special starvation diet, or if I have spent time in a special clinic. There have even been rumours about plastic surgery or even a serious illness! Well, let me assure you, there has been nothing so dramatic in my life.

So what is the answer? What is my secret? It is not magic, or some kind of trick - my health is not a subject I would joke about.

I lost weight thanks to the knowledge shared with me by my dear Swiss friend, Anne-Marie, someone I met at a time when my weight was at its highest and I was at my lowest. Anne-Marie is a nutrition specialist - her approach to healthy weight loss is a gentle and sensible method, based on common sense.

Does it really matter what we look like? Yes, I think it does...

Why do we all have such a great need for our appearance to be "acceptable to society"? I guess if we are honest with ourselves it is because we all do appreciate compliments and who is not pleased when we see appreciation of our looks reflected in the eyes of others? Surely very few of us.

We spend a significant part of our lives looking - consciously or unconsciously - for acceptance by other people. Just a smile or a positive comment can make us feel good about ourselves. Sometimes we can be too proud to admit, even to ourselves, that admiration, friendship, affection and love are the things that make us happy.

To gain the acceptance of others we often have to conform to the rules which society also follows. And if we think we can make our own rules and live according to them, we have to bow to a greater power - the opinion of society. Nonconformists attract the attention of others for a short time, but this usually has nothing to do with admiration or acceptance, just curiosity.

People are basically good, those things which are regarded as best usually are best, and because love really is the key to happiness, we should not regard the idea of "conformity" negatively because it means fitting in with these ideals.

Society demands a great deal from us and it places great value on beauty, a yardstick that allows comparisons and judgements to be made. That which pleases the eye attracts attention and beauty has become a synonym for other desirable attributes, too.

During the last few decades advertising has to a great extent contributed to the increased value placed upon beauty and good looks and the best results here are obtained by those experts who know just what appeals to most people. Advertising hoardings and screens bombard us with beauty and this bombardment influences our expectations.

We are not capable of avoiding continual assessment, unless we have decided upon a peculiar, hermit-like life without love. We don't differ much from one-another when it comes to wanting to be admired, loved and appreciated. We all like to make a good impression. When we are fat, we don't feel this is possible. That is why...

"WE DON'T WANT TO BE FAT ..."

My Method

As you have already read, the weight-loss method I suggest in this book is based on good sound common sense. Why? Because nature is perfect and balanced and our bodies are a part of nature. If you give your body a good supply of what it needs, it will reward you with a balanced figure.

How can we give our organism this balance? Here lies the secret of my method, which I will now reveal to readers who have decided to reduce weight in an intelligent, healthy way in harmony with nature. You will certainly be astounded at how uncomplicated it actually is! You will also be astounded at the changes your body will go through. Don't get carried away though with simply reading about the simplicity of this method - to lose unwanted kilos and to feel good about yourself again you can't just limit yourself to reading a book. You also have to follow the instructions contained within the book.

You may find it worthwhile to read the book through several times - keep it handy (not difficult, given its size) so you can have a quick read if you need some encouragement - and never give up trying. You can and you will regain your lost figure, just as I did. At the same time your well being will be radically improved, too. What could be nicer than to once again arouse people's admiration? All of us, men and women, need to know we look good. Why deny it?

I will now describe the method that has proven so very successful for me. Like all of Mother Nature's laws, this method is based on a few important rules. I look upon these rules as commandments - because I feel we should live our lives according to them. There are ten of these commandments all of which can be included in one axiom of fundamental importance. This is:

*"We can only achieve balance when we live in harmony with our bodies and our intellect. If we try to separate these two parts of our being - body and mind - then we will never achieve harmony. No amount of diets, methods or training can enable us to achieve long-term loss of our superfluous kilos if we don't respect the necessary natural balance. For this reason the most important focus of my method is not on an actual slimming diet but - on the contrary - **it is the enjoyment of food which will mark the beginning of your new slim figure.**"*

Maggie's Ten Commandments:

Look after your mind:
1. Make peace with yourself.
2. Be aware of your body's needs.
3. Use relaxation techniques.
4. Be certain of success.
5. Live according to the rules of the art of weight reduction.

Provide for your body by eating what you feel like
6. Devise a healthy rhythm of life for a healthy body.
7. Follow some very simple rules concerning nutrition.
8. Be aware of what you eat.
9. Don't forget the seasoning.
10. Drink green tea

Part 1:

Look after your mind

The first five commandments which I will talk about in Part I may have little to do with food, but they are the keys to success. Trust me. By keeping to these commandments you will lose weight in a natural and lasting way.

The First Commandment

Make peace with yourself

As I began to explain earlier, you first have to tidy up your own mind in order to lose weight. You must learn to respect and love yourself, stop fighting your internal battles and make peace with yourself. This is something I fully understand because I was very stressed and uptight when I started waging unnecessary war against the extra kilos. If we force our bodies into constraints completely against nature, we cause ourselves so much stress and strain. Then your body will revolt and revenge itself, like any living thing.

The only way to lose weight without fighting against yourself is to do it in reconciliation with yourself, with respect for your own body and mind.

It is important that you do not spend too much time constantly thinking and worrying about being overweight - do not become obsessive. On the contrary, you should make an effort not to torment yourself, as this will bring you no peace. It's best to look at yourself positively. Tell yourself:
"I will stop fighting against myself"
" I deserve to have fun."
" I will never again sit down at the table feeling guilty."
"When I sit down to eat I will feel happy."
"I will enjoy every meal without haste."

Learn to accept your own body and not to systematically punish yourself because you are eating. You should eat - *you have to eat!* Eating is one of life's normal functions. You should never feel guilty about nourishing yourself. You only have to teach your own body how to make use of the supply of nutrition according to its metabolism.

The Second Commandment

Be aware of your body's needs

Self-knowledge is vital. In order to grow in the maturity needed to be able to reduce weight, you have to have full knowledge of your own body and mind. You should get to know them - their strengths and weaknesses. Take responsibility for what you perceive as your advantages and disadvantages. Becoming self-aware is a crucial step on the road to a better figure.

Self-analysis can be quite difficult, so I suggest you start with something quite easy - as I did - in order to cast out your own demons. There is one very effective aid to this process - a mirror!

Choose a place in your home where nobody will disturb you (and a time!) and hang a large mirror on the wall. Take off your clothes and stand completely naked in front of the mirror. Look at yourself carefully, examine every part of your body, get used to your body and accept it. Don't reject it after your first glance in the mirror - examine any feelings that may arise - and remember you will be getting slimmer. By truly facing up to yourself you **will** achieve so much and be so proud of yourself.

Your mind can work miracles, it can be your greatest ally - but not when it is stressed and confused, then it can be your greatest enemy. The subconscious influences not only the physiological functioning of the body but *everything* we do. It is revealed mainly through imagination. Imagination can stop us from achieving if we do not learn to control it. Think about it, most of our fears for the future are actually just imagination running riot - the future doesn't even exist yet, so why waste time worrying?

If we placed a 20 metre long, 40 centimetre wide plank at a height of 20 centimetres from the ground, most of us would have no problem walking, or even running, from one end of it to the other. Yet if we were to place the same plank from one 5th floor balcony to another we would surely have trouble finding a volunteer to even walk along it. Why? You would probably say acrophobia (the fear of falling from a great height), but it actually has more to do with your imagination calling up something called autosuggestion. You would start telling your-self all that could go wrong - your imagination would run riot.

We expend so much energy worrying and waste a great deal of our time thanks to unconscious autosuggestion of this kind. It is wise to learn conscious autosuggestion and how to control our imagination to create a positive affect. We are what we eat - and we are also what we think...

If you are convinced you really do want to lose weight, then you will lose weight - I am the proof. However, your imagination is not easily duped - it is not stupid and requires wisely chosen information. In order to walk along the plank, be it twenty centimetres or twenty metres high, you first have to learn how to place one foot in front of the other. Chunk things down, take it one step at a time and curb your imagination.

Dig out a picture of yourself that was taken while you were slim, or maybe even a picture of a person you aspire to looking like. Firmly impress this picture into your memory, so it will still be there even while you sleep. Let your imagination see you looking just that way in the future, rather than conjuring up worried pictures of you looking the same or even fatter than you are now - be in control of your destiny.

Now, back to that mirror. Be objective when you look at your reflection, this is not an exercise in destructive self-criticism. Comments such as: "I am, I always was and will always be a nobody," are not helpful. But don't be too lenient either, pacifying yourself with arguments such as: "Well some people like me the way I am." Who are you trying to convince? What do you really want? **Be honest with yourself**. Just take a sensible and healthy look at 'you' and make a decision to change 'you' for the better - to become slim.

Certainly autosuggestion by itself is not enough to make you reduce weight fast. Food alone is also not enough. The transformation will consist of several factors at least.

One way to help the whole process is to calm your mind and your body - and in order to do this you should pay attention to how you breathe. Correct breathing increases your energy, cleanses your body, improves your thinking processes, increases your stamina, calms your mind and generally revitalises your whole system - even helping to make your skin clearer and brighter. What better way to help motivate you to lose weight?

Standing in front of your mirror is a great place to practise some breathing exercises. More often than not our breathing is too shallow - we don't take in enough oxygen or expel enough stale air. Spend a while concentrating only on your breathing and discover how you breathe. Now, take a long slow breath that starts deep down in your lungs and fills your whole body. Hold it for a moment, then breathe out slowly - every last bit of air. When did you last take a breath like that? *

Next, breathe in and push out your tummy at the same time - it should feel as if you were being blown up like a balloon. Feel your chest broadening as you do this. Hold your breath for a moment, and then slowly breathe out while gradually pulling your diaphragm in as much as possible. Feel how this empties your lungs. Now try it again, slowly and calmly. Aim to repeat this every day for three to five minutes.

(*NOTE:
If you should start to feel at all dizzy while doing your breathing exercises, stop, sit down and don't try it again until the following day.)

In order to achieve harmony between your mind and your body it is not necessary to go deep into yoga techniques, but it is worthwhile pointing out that the breathing exercises which derive from yoga can be very helpful.

The Third Commandment

Use Relaxation Techniques

Relaxation techniques used regularly can be a valuable help to you in reaching your correct weight. For me, learning to relax helped to free my mind of the demons tormenting it. As I began to truly relax my body and soul became open to new life possibilities and the less I worried about my weight and my figure. The less I worried, the slimmer I became.

Relaxation is enhanced by the right surroundings and it is worth taking a bit of time and trouble to create your own little oasis. Find a room in which you can place a few plants (best of all would be the room where you have hung your big mirror). An indoor garden, even a small one, will bring your home life and energy. A corner where nature predominates will give you the feeling of being in harmony with your surroundings and thus with your inner being.

If there is no fireplace in this room where you could light a fire - or if it is too warm - try lighting some candles instead. Such natural light has a tremendous calming influence. Fire or candlelight is also flattering to your naked reflection in the mirror, making it easier to imagine your new, sensuous, slim figure. So is great for enhancing your visualisation.

Once you have created an environment that will aid relaxation, you must learn to relax and to recuperate properly. Your body will so appreciate these moments of genuine relaxation and will let you know by more easily eliminating the toxins that have accumulated during the course of the day.

"How do I reach a state of complete relaxation?"

In our day and age the ability to attain true relaxation and tranquillity is a rare gift. Words like "effort", "work", "frustration", "nervousness", "tension" and "stress" are often heard. Yet how seldom do we hear the expressions "peace", "mental balance" or "harmony"? It seems at times as if a positive way of looking at life in our present, complicated world has become almost impossible.

Reaching a state of total relaxation requires practise. Giving yourself an 'order' to recuperate will not make you relax, you have to work at it. Find a comfy spot in your little oasis (a bed, sofa, pillows, or even just a nice soft carpet), lie down and try to let go of all the tensions in your body. When you feel you cannot relax any more, mentally check through your body to see how much your muscles have actually relaxed. Perhaps some of your muscles are halfway relaxed? To clarify this, starting with your toe muscles and slowly moving up the body towards the head (not forgetting to relax your scalp) try to increase the degree of relaxation in each and every muscle. I am sure you will be able to.

Become like a rag doll, let your legs sink into the bed/sofa/floor, make them feel really heavy and lifeless. Feel your body getting softer and relaxed. Nothing is keeping it in this place; it is just there, that is all. Your hands and your arms are getting heavy. You neck is no longer being supported by muscles, your head is lying motionless on the pillow. Your eyes are closed. You are really relaxed.

In this rag doll state you will feel pleasant sensations. Peace comes. You feel shielded from the world and your nearest surroundings. In fact it wouldn't take much to send you to sleep. Hold on to this state of complete peace, at the same time remaining quietly aware of each part of your body, so that it does not tense up. Stay like that for a while.

Think about each part of your body in turn. If you feel you can without disturbing your peace gently raise your legs a few centimetres from the mattress and feel how heavy they are when they fall back down. Imagine you are apart from your body - drifting off somewhere as if asleep. None of your muscles are tense. Starting with your feet, examine in your mind your calves, knees, thighs - can they relax any further? Then check your hands, right down to the fingertips - do they feel soft, unable to hold anything?

Many people find the neck and head the most difficult parts to relax, but with perseverance you can do it. Let your head sink into the pillow and check your face muscles, too. Unclench your jaw, relax your eyebrows and your forehead and let your tongue lie naturally at the bottom of your mouth behind your teeth - holding it up on the roof of your mouth will create tension in your neck.

The advantages of relaxation

Learning relaxation techniques will enable you to repress your worries and cares until they are completely gone. Harmful habits and emotions will disappear and make room for a feeling of harmony and joie de vivre. Your relaxed body will no longer send negative information to your brain and as a result you will gradually lose your faulty behaviour patterns. You will see life in a new light.

Relaxation allows your consciousness to gain a new, deeper dimension, empowering you to fulfil your most secret dreams. It will prepare you to confront the problem you have long wanted to solve - the shedding of superfluous weight. A relaxed body knows how to nourish itself in a healthy, balanced and fulfilling way.

The Fourth Commandment

Be Certain of Success

Here I should like to say a few more words about autosuggestion - as already mentioned in the second commandment. This somewhat complicated expression relates to the most certain and at the same time simplest way to attain the total conviction that you can lose weight.

It is at this stage that you will lay the foundation stone for your future nutrition. It will be healthy and of great use to you. With the aid of autosuggestion you will convince yourself that you actually will lose weight *without* losing your enjoyment of food.

In the first stage you will visualise the ideal figure you dream about. The most effective way of doing this is to find a photo of a slim you, or a person you most want to look like and to replace their face with a photo of your face. The more often you call this picture to mind, the better your results will be. Place this picture somewhere prominent and keep looking at it.

In the second stage you will visualise the foods you find most irresistible, i.e. those which are the cause of your weight problem (cakes, sweets, biscuits, fatty snacks etc). Next, associate these dishes with names like "bitter", "poison" or "danger". After repeating this exercise several times, you will find to your amazement that you will feel a genuine aversion towards the very foods that once made your mouth water.

Follow these two essential stages - first visualising the body you want, then labelling the forbidden foods - and you will not feel any of the frustration so often experienced when you go on a strict diet. On the contrary, you will feel immense satisfaction at the victory you have won over yourself! You will also be full of hope, because you know you can achieve the figure you have dreamed of. You are already on the way...

It is amazing how much your eating habits will change. You will experience nothing but pleasure in preparing and trying the meals that will lead to an effortless loss of pounds.

Affirmations

I would like to share with you another of my secrets that will add to your autosuggestion sessions. These are the words that I repeated to myself every evening before going to sleep:

"I am getting slimmer step by step. I will be slim and look like the new picture I have of myself. I will enjoy eating healthily, eating vegetables, lean meat and fruit and will get slimmer and slimmer. I will not eat sweets, biscuits, greasy sausages, fatty cheeses or bread. I will lose all the weight I want to lose. I will be loved and admired."

Of course you can make up some affirmations of your own, the exact words you use do not matter as long as there is meaning behind the words. Repeat your affirmations every day, ideally at the same time each day.

The Fifth Commandment

Live according to the rules of the art of weight reduction

This commandment is actually a summary of the four preceding ones. By now you should understand that it is pointless to torture your body because if you do that you will be in constant conflict with it. Your mind must be ready to accept that you will lose weight. Only then can you lose weight and keep it off and earn the figure that you would like to keep until the end of your life.

Once you have decided to follow the method that proved so very successful for me, you have made the decision to get rid of your superfluous kilos *forever*. You have decided to finally devote yourself to your 'self' - because <u>you are worth it.</u>

Stop blaming yourself for the times you were defeated while trying all kinds of different diets in the past. It was not your fault. No diet or slimming treatment can work if it is used without emotional and mental preparation.

Of course these first five commandments are not sufficient to get you slim, but they are the basis for your further action. It is time to devote yourself to yourself - of course your children/partner/parents need you - but you need you too!

When did you last treat yourself? Well now is the time to do it! Find time for yourself, not only for eating, but also for living. How about running yourself a pampering bath filled with herbs and scented oils? Give yourself a facial, manicure and pedicure - have a real 'girlie' night in and spoil yourself. Go and treat yourself to a course of massage or learn the techniques of self-massage (there are plenty of great self-help books out there). Massage is great for ridding your body of toxins, tension and stress.

Take yourself out for a walk and take note of the beauty around you. If you like sports start to jog, swim or cycle regularly - anything aerobic will increase your metabolic weight, even after you have finished exercising, making you feel just great. Perhaps you would prefer a short session of aerobics to music. Do whatever suits you, something that is fun - it should not be a chore or a pain. Start slowly and you will be surprised at the results.

Occupying yourself like this will not only use energy and burn fat, but it will also give you the mental energy you need to lose weight. Besides, when you are enjoying yourself, you will not be thinking about your weight or about the need to lose it - you will simply be feeling good. Once you have found inner harmony you will no longer feel the need to compensate by eating.

Let us now go to the problems connected with the body itself. Here there are also five very simple rules that you should follow.

Part 2:

Care for your body by eating what you like

In part 2 I would like to draw your attention not only to what you eat, but how you eat. It won't be a lecture about strict dieting or a slimming regimen; I will only try to introduce you to a few rules that we should keep to in our nutrition. All the rules that I have presented in the form of commandments are based on common sense and the will to live a healthy lifestyle.

If you keep to these rules you will get the figure of your dreams and in addition will be brimming with energy for life. You will enjoy such a wonderful feeling of well being and you will look great - as never before. Even your skin, hair and nails will look better - you will be shining with vitality. That is exactly what happened to me, and it is waiting for you. You want to lose weight and I want to help you - so let's get to work!

The Sixth Commandment

Devise a healthy rhythm of life for a healthy body

Ask yourself the following questions:

- How many meals do I eat a day?

- How often during the day do I nibble something or snack between meals?

- Can I remember in detail what I ate during the previous day?

- And if not, why can't I remember?

- What do I feel when I see food?

Then make up a list in which you note down everything you ate yesterday. <u>Don't leave anything out</u>, remember every snack, every sweet, and every biscuit that you grabbed during the day and quickly ate.

When you have completed your list, the time has come to have an honest, truthful discussion with yourself about your relationship with food. Why you eat... how often you eat... what you eat - think carefully about it so you finally understand how you feed yourself and why you do it that way and not any other. Be absolutely honest! This is so important and you may well be surprised with the results!

Three large meals

There is nothing wrong with eating three main meals a day, but you have to admit that often these meals are too substantial, which is why you gain weight. Three daily meals of a sensible size will give you enough nutrition and allow you to lose weight, especially if eaten at the right times.

If your greatest physical or mental efforts are needed during the morning, you should never go without a nutritious breakfast. A cup of coffee drunk as you prepare for work is not enough and will only leave you wanting to snack mid-morning, if not sooner! Your breakfast doesn't have to be a sumptuous feast, but you should make sure that it contains all the necessary nutrients - paying special attention to protein.

Your daily rhythm can decide whether you take your main meal at midday or in the evening. It does not matter too much, especially when your choice of foodstuff and the amount is kept within sensible limits.

Snacks

Between meals there are moments when you may have an irres- istible urge to eat something. And if you are anything like I was - in most cases you will give way to this urge and end up eating some- thing unhealthy. Let me tell you, there are *very few people* who have actually gained weight because they ate three meals a day! Most of us got fat by continual nibbling and munching between meals.

Come on be honest: Do you satisfy your hunger with a little snack two hours after breakfast? Do you take an active part in your children's lunch? Do you nibble biscuits while you work? Is every cup of tea or coffee accompanied by a few biscuits? Do you often snack in front of the television or, even worse, in bed? Do you maybe even manage a fourth meal late at night - because if you do you can be sure it is in someway responsible for those fat thighs!

It is very easy to change these habits when you harmoniously create meals that provide your body with everything it needs. It is even easier to go without snacks when you understand how bad the consequences of such habits can be. When you do decide to change your habits, do it gradually, not all at once. Start by cutting down on your snacks and maybe try replacing cakes, chocolates and sweets with healthier options, such as fruit, raw vegetables, or maybe a few nuts or dried fruits. Then slowly phase them out, too.

A little bit here, a little bit there

Nibbling between meals does so much harm. In fact we are often almost unaware we are doing it, it becomes automatic to have a bite here, crunch something there. Maybe you snack when preparing a meal, or clearing up the dishes after the kids have eaten (whose children don't have leftovers on their plates?) or while out shopping. We are often not conscious of how much we are actually consuming at these times. But add all these snacks together and they probably equal one or two unnecessary meals each day! Re-read the list you made showing everything you ate yesterday and check whether you are giving into this kind of temptation.

The Seventh Commandment

Follow some very simple rules of nutrition

Do not combine certain foods

For many years there has been a method which thousands of people all over the world have confirmed as effective. It is based on eating protein products (meat, eggs, and cheese) separately from carbohydrates (pastries, rice, pasta, and potatoes) and only eating fruits with other fruits. (Raw or cooked vegetables can and indeed should be eaten with both carbohydrates and proteins)

Let's have a look at the basic rules of this method...

If we only eat to satisfy our hunger and our metabolism is normal, there is no reason why we should gain weight. If we are too fat, this means we are eating the wrong foods, the wrong combinations of foods or simply too much. Restoration of the correct dietary balance is enough for us to start losing weight.

A malfunctioning digestive system can be the cause of fatness, because it makes it impossible for the body to correctly utilise the nourishment it receives. The wrong combination of foods inhibits correct digestion. For instance, carbohydrates are broken down first by enzymes present in our saliva, while proteins are broken down by acids in our stomach. Now, because stomach acids stop the activity of the saliva, it is not possible to digest protein and carbohydrates at the same time.

Let's imagine for instance what happens when we eat meat with rice:

- The meat reaches the stomach where it is exposed to the effects of the stomach acids that begin to break down the proteins.
- Meanwhile the rice mixes with our saliva before reaching the stomach, where the stomach acids, which are busy working on the meat protein, stop the saliva from functioning.
- This interrupts the digestion of the rice that then starts fermenting and can lead to toxic substances being formed.
- So, a meal consisting of meat and rice (protein and carbohydrate) cannot be properly used by our body and can contribute to fatness.

Tip:
In order to make the process of digestion easier; all foods should be chewed thoroughly.

Fruits, which consist of water, cellulose and sugar, are not digested until they reach the small intestine. When eaten with protein or carbohydrates they are stopped in the stomach, where they start to ferment. So again, **fruits should always be eaten separately**.

Green vegetables, rich in vitamins and minerals, are essential for the correct digestion and absorption of proteins. They also have a positive influence on the carbohydrate metabolism. If they are missing from the diet they can cause nutritional deficiencies - so this is why **green vegetables should always accompany both carbohydrate and protein meals**.

Fats are neutral, but they do slow down the digestion process and place an unnecessary burden on it, so are best eaten in small quantities.

Here are 4 rules concerning food combining:

1. After eating a meal consisting of proteins you should wait four hours before eating any carbohydrates.

2. After eating a meal rich in carbohydrates you should wait four hours before you eat a meal containing proteins or fruits.

3. After eating a meal consisting of fruit you should wait two hours before you eat foods containing carbohydrates.

4. If a meal containing protein or carbohydrates consists of over 30 percent fat, you should wait seven hours before eating anything at all.

Here's a summary of the rules:

1. Proteins can be combined with vegetables, but not with carbohydrates.

2. Carbohydrates can be combined with vegetables, but not with proteins.

3. Fat slows down the digestion process.

4. Fruits can only be combined with other fruits.

The following combinations are therefore <u>forbidden:</u>

- Bread with cheese, meat, fish or eggs,
- Pasta with cheese, meat, fish or eggs,
- Rice with cheese, meat, fish or eggs,
- Potatoes with cheese, meat, fish or eggs,
- Pancakes and ravioli with cheese, meat, fish or eggs,
- Only eat limited amounts of beans, lentils and peas.

<u>Add some bran to your meals</u>

Indigestible plant fibres are (as their name suggests) not digested and are therefore eliminated without being processed. One of their main advantages is that they actually accelerate the movement of the residues from the metabolic process through the last part of the digestive tract and facilitate the excretion of waste products.

Until the beginning of the 20th-century plant fibres were underestimated because they did not supply any calories. Foods were at that time assessed on their energy value alone. It was not until much later that plant fibres aroused interest because of their anti-constipation effect. It was found that the more compact the food (in connection with increased consumption of meat, milk, sugar, eggs and fat), the more necessary plant fibres were to facilitate their passage through the intestines. Later it was also discovered that plant fibres absorb a lot of water and expand, making you feel fuller and delaying the onset of hunger.

Because they accelerate the passage of food through the intestines, they also prevent metabolic residues from staying too long in the large intestine and harming the intestinal walls. In this way they help to hinder intestinal cancer. They are also an excellent prophylactic against disorders of the flow of bile, because they can absorb bile salts and cholesterol.

Tip:
Everyone who wants to lose weight and to improve his or her health should eat plenty of fibre.

Plant fibres are found in the skins of fruit, in seeds, seaweed, green vegetables, barley pods and therefore also in **bran** - which is how I recommend you eat it. Bran can be bought in most supermarkets and can be sprinkled on your meals or added to sauces. It is difficult to judge exactly how much plant fibre you should give your body every day, but it is certain that most people suffer from a lack. It is therefore wise to include bran in our daily nutrition. I use it all the time and it really does not spoil the flavour of other foods.

Start by eating one spoonful of bran every day, split into two portions and added to your two main meals. Step by step increase the dose every three days to two, three, then four spoonfuls a day. Four spoonfuls a day are ideal. Believe me - it works!

Vegetables are one of our body's best friends.
Experiment with vegetables in your diet and you will get to know the way they work. They not only make natural weight loss easier, because they provide satisfying bulk as well as lots of essential nutrients, but they also make you feel brighter and healthier. They have a positive effect on your skin and their healing powers are very soon visible with a clearer and brighter complexion.

Diuretic vegetables are particularly useful and should be eaten often (every meal if possible) and in unlimited quantities. They aid the digestion process and increase the rate at which you lose weight and excrete water. Below is a list of vegetables with diuretic properties:
• Carrots
• Celery
• Chicory

- Cucumbers
- Watercress
- Dill
- Green salad
- Onions
- Sorrel
- Leek
- Potatoes
- Goat's beard
- Tomatoes
- Artichokes.

Don't forget liquids

Water is the source of life - in fact most of our body is actually composed of water - thanks to which we can enjoy good health and a slim, attractive figure. Not drinking enough water can lead to lethargy and many other health complaints, such as headaches and mood swings, so you really should be sure to drink enough. The recommended amount is at least two litres every day. Drink this amount and you will feel and look so much healthier.

Note, however, that you should only drink between meals. Avoid drinking during meals, because this can lead to digestive disorders. Drinking between meals does have another advantage, too - it appeases hunger. Health experts claim that we often mistake our bodies thirst for hunger - so next time you feel hungry, try drinking some water before you turn to the food cupboard. It mat well be that you are only thirsty...

The Eighth Commandment

Be aware of what you eat

Vegetables with edible seeds (beans, peas, lentils) often have a higher nutritional value than fleshy plants, and they also contain nuclein and lecithin which provide our bodies with large amounts of easily assimilated phosphorus. But they all have one disadvantage - the sugar they contain ferments in the stomach. For this reason it is recommended to combine them with vegetables which have a diuretic and laxative effect, or with bran which will reduce the negative results of eating this type of vegetable.

Edible parts of vegetables:

Buds or young shoots (asparagus, artichokes, white cabbage)
Tubers (potatoes)
Bulbs (onions, leeks, garlic)
Roots (carrots, beetroots, salsify)
Leaves (sorrel, spinach, chicory and all kinds of salad)
Seeds (beans, peas, lentils)
Fruit (pumpkin, cucumber, squash, courgettes)

Fresh vegetables are less nutritious than dried vegetables when compared weight by weight, but fresh vegetables provide the body with large amounts of water. Fresh and dried vegetables are packed with minerals such as potassium oxalate, sodium oxalate, magnesium oxalate and iron oxalate, plus iron nitrate and iron citrate which are essential for our tissues. Vegetables complement meat in more ways than one, because mineral salts also compensate for the acidifying effect of meat dishes!

Note:
Asparagus, beets and cabbage have the highest content of nitrate substances.
Beetroots, carrots and onions have the highest sugar content.

Nutrients from vegetables with edible leaves are contained in substances called cellulose compounds, of which only a small part is absorbed by our body. The parts that cannot be absorbed control the transport of the food through the intestines, so preventing constipation, which, believe it or not, is a major contributory factor to corpulence in many people. So it's easy to understand why it is worthwhile eating lots of fresh vegetables ... ideally enriched with bran!

Tips for cooking vegetables

As you probably know, the process of cooking significantly reduces the nutritional value of most foods, especially vegetables, so it is wise to take care of 'how' you cook.

Globulin, along with calcium oxide and magnesium oxide, forms compounds that are insoluble in water. For this reason vegetables can actually get harder if cooked in water containing a lot of calcium. To avoid this, add sodium carbonate (4-5 gr. per litre) to the water and this will absorb the insoluble salts. (If you do not have any sodium carbonate, then use common salt, the results are similar).

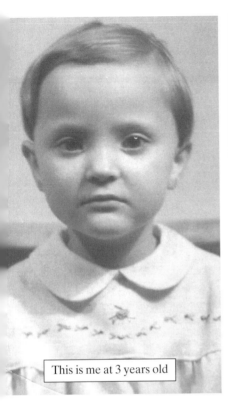

This is me at 3 years old

At kindergarten I already knew I would be an actress

With the girl guides in the congress hall

Playing the parrot in "Czupurek" directed by Adam Hanuszkiewicz

In the play "Czaber z Gabra" directed by Adam Hanuszkiewicz

Class reunion at Michal Bajor's (from left: Maria Gladkowska, Mali Drotz, Agnieszka Kotulanka, Marek Robaczewski

A banquet at my home

With Adam Hanuszkiweicz during the filming of a television play

The Nowy Theatre ensemble

Holidaying in sunny Tunisia

Skiing holiday in Van Thorens

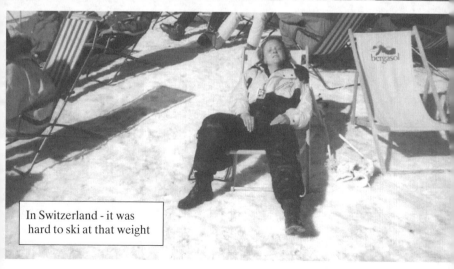

In Switzerland - it was
hard to ski at that weight

Spain - I just couldn't ignore those food shops ....

... especially when there were such delicious sausages to be had

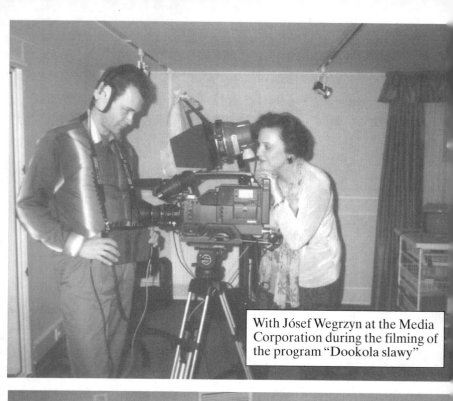

With Jósef Wegrzyn at the Media Corporation during the filming of the program "Dookola slawy"

How my adventures with synchronisation started (a photo of the recording session at Master Film)

Class reunion at Michal Bajor's

With Iza Trojanowska during the filming of the first episodes of "Clan"

At my house after the première of "One week in the life of a man" by Jerry Stuhr

Do not forget that green vegetables are very tender. The water-soluble nutrients they contain are lost when the vegetables are placed in cold water and then heated. In order to conserve as many nutrients as possible cook your vegetables in the minimum amount of water - or even better, steam them instead. And don't waste the nutrient rich water after straining your vegetables - use it to prepare stocks, soups or sauces.

Ideally vegetables should be placed into boiling salted water so that the albumin they contain coagulates quickly. An exception to this is potatoes cooked in their skins, because they will be protected by their skin during the cooking process. Fresh, delicate tasting vegetables are best served slightly cooked and crunchy, because if cooked for too long they will lose their flavour and aroma.

Green vegetables such as spinach, sorrel, runner beans and artichokes can sometimes frustratingly turn yellow during cooking. In order to retain their fresh green colour, place them into fast boiling water and cook them uncovered, then refresh with cold water and drain.

White vegetables such as cauliflower will stay white if cooked uncovered and at a relatively low heat. One centuries-old method of cooking, and one which I recommend to you, is to add one spoonful of flour and a little vinegar to the water when cooking them - this will ensure that they stay white and firm and makes them taste delicious, too.

Food preparation

The flavour of most foods is enhanced when they are prepared simply. It is so worthwhile discovering the real taste of what you are eating, rather than disguising it or losing it through complicated processes.

For example:

- When preparing meat, roast it rather than braise it and while it's roasting, baste with vegetable stock instead of meat stock.

- When you boil meat, always put it into boiling water, never cold. The meat will then taste better and the broth will contain fewer calories.

- Animal and plant fats are - contrary to common opinion - more easily digested cold or slightly warmed. (It is not toxic, but be careful, fat is harmful to health when heated above 150°C.)

- Eat wholemeal bread, not white (though you do not have to completely exclude white bread from your diet) and use wholemeal flour when baking.

Below is a list of foods that I consider to be my "Slimming Friends". It is well worth eating these more frequently:

Brussels sprouts
Celery
Cucumber
Leek
Chicory
Spinach
Dill
Cabbage
Cauliflower
Pumpkin
Radishes
Soya
Green Salad
Artichokes

Asparagus
Mushrooms
Pineapple
Lemons
Grapefruit
Oranges
Apples
Strawberries
Melons
Tofu
Low-fat quark (ricotta)
Low-fat yoghurt
Eggs
Chicken (without skin)
Turkey (without skin)
Fish
Seafood

Finally, I want to share with you the recipe for my delicious and healthy slimming broth. You can drink it, baste your meat with it, or even add it to sauces instead of water or fat.

Slimming Broth recipe:

Ingredients:
2 carrots (peeled as thinly as possible so as not to lose the valuable vitamins hidden just under the skin)
2 leeks
1 celery
1 sprig of parsley
1 onion studded with cloves

Method:
Place the vegetables in a large pot and cover with a large amount of cold water, and then boil for three hours. Next, add a

little salt, strain the mixture and fill the pot with water until you have two litres of liquid.

Note:
You will certainly have noticed that the rules for cooking vegetables have been broken in this recipe! Because most of their nutrients will have leached out into the water - but don't forget, in this instance we are interested in the broth, not the vegetables.

(Any broth not used immediately should be stored in the refrigerator.)

The Ninth Commandment

Don't forget the seasoning

Seasonings are aromatic substances obtained from the bark, roots, pods, fruits and seeds of a number of plants. They come from all continents of the world and are added to various foods to improve their flavour or to make them more easily digestible. They also do something that is of particular importance to anyone wishing to lose weight - *they actually stimulate the functioning of the digestive system!*

Below are a number of seasonings you can put to good use in your kitchen - combining the useful with the pleasurable. Those I personally use most often are: pepper, nutmeg, cinnamon, paprika, coriander, vanilla, cloves, basil, mint, thyme, bay leaves, dill, aniseed, caraway, dried onions and garlic. Of course you can amend this selection according to your own taste and preferences.

Tip:
Seasoning should never be overdone, since it can lead to digestive disorders! Use them in moderation.

Anise
Fruits are used for cakes, infusions and herbal teas. It is good for easing cramps, so helps stomach pains, flatulence, and colic and aids the digestion.

Basil

Found mostly in Mediterranean countries, where it is a common ingredient in food preparation. It is especially good for seasoning courgettes, aubergines and tomatoes. Basil eases cramps and stomach pains and aids the digestion. It also has an antibacterial effect.

Tarragon

Tarragon is mainly used in sauce preparation, but is also useful to season salads, eggs, chicken and mussels. It supports the digestion and soothes the stomach.

Caraway

Caraway comes from the same family as carrots, anise and dill. Like all the plants in this family it has diuretic properties and stimulates the digestive process. It improves the taste of cheese and is a valuable component of any curry dish.

Dill

This is related to anise. Its leaves and fruits improve the flavour of fish, salads or cucumbers. Dill has a positive effect on the elimination of wind, is diuretic, supports the digestion and eases cramps.

Parsley

Has a diuretic and tonic effect and is very rich in vitamin C and minerals.

Rosemary

Great for improving the flavour of roast dishes! Rosemary stimulates the functions of the liver and elimination of bile. It was also the main ingredient in the water used by the Hungarian queen as a Balm of Eternal Youth!

Sage

Improves the flavour of poultry and all tomato dishes and supports the digestion.

Sorrel

Its sour taste improves the taste of many meats and it is also often used in egg and chicken dishes. It has a mildly diuretic and laxative effect. *However, Sorrel is not recommended for people suffering from stomach ulcers, arthritis, rheumatism or urinary problems.*

Chervil

Especially good chopped in salads and soups. Has a diuretic, laxative effect.

Thyme

An ideal herb for broth, soups, pies and fillings of all kinds - and also added to carrots. Is generally considered as a bactericide. Supports the cleansing of the body and sweating, has a positive effect on the digestion and the elimination of wind.

Cinnamon

Stimulates the digestion and strengthens. Hot wine with cinnamon or cinnamon tea is a useful remedy for flu or colds.

Cloves

An ideal addition to meat and sauce, cloves can also be used in the preparation of desserts. A powerful bactericide, cloves also prevent flatulence.

Pepper

White and black pepper pleasantly stimulate the nose and are suitable for very many dishes (meat, fish or salads). Pepper has a significant healing effect, supporting the digestion and stimulating the body's functions.

The chewing of peppercorns causes more saliva to be produced, releasing a great amount of enzymes which begin to digest many proteins and sugars while they are still in the mouth. Pepper is also said to be an aphrodisiac!

Ginger

Forms quite delicious blends with either sweet or savoury foods. A well-known strengthening, digestion-stimulating spice which also prevents flatulence. In China and the Philippines it is served as an infusion instead of coffee. After a heavy meal it can prevent nausea, while supporting the metabolism and preventing constipation. In China it has been found that ginger improves the sight when used for a long time, so is often used as a component in sight-improving medications.

In phytotherapy ginger is prescribed as an aid to digestion in the form of easy to take gelatine capsules. It can also be taken as a tincture, in a one to five dilution, with 20-30 drops to be taken before each meal. Research has also shown that ginger helps to reduce the levels of cholesterol in the blood.

Coriander

Enhances the taste of cooked vegetables and salads. Has a positive effect on the digestion and elimination of wind.

Turmeric (Indian Saffron)

This spice is the basis for most traditional Indian curries. Increases the output of bile, thus supporting the digestion. It is also said to be stimulating and strongly diuretic. Can be used as an infusion or decoction - 5 gr. per litre of water (two cups to be drunk every day).

Cardamom

This plant grows mainly in southern India and is used in the Near East and in North Africa to improve the flavour of coffee. The Chinese consider it a unique cure-all. It is said to prevent faintness caused by digestive disorders. Chemical analyses show that cardamom contains lipase, a fat reducing enzyme.

Bay Leaves

Used whole, added to stews or casseroles, bay leaves have a distinctive delicious aroma. Contains an essence that stimulates the output of bile and thus facilitates the process of digestion. This herb should be used in moderation.

Nutmeg

Nutmeg was brought by the Dutch from the Molucca Islands (Spice Islands) and first appeared in Europe in the 18th century. Its mild aroma and delicate taste allow it to be used to season a great many dishes - particularly improving the taste of vegetable soups and egg or cheese dishes. It aids the digestion of hard to digest foods by stimulating the digestive system.

Paprika

Since it was introduced to Europe in 1932, paprika has been recognised as containing a great amount of vitamin C (0.1 - 0.5%, depending on the variety). It is considered to be a stimulant, and also has a positive effect on the digestive process and is a very good anti-flatulent. In days gone by people used to place pieces of paprika inside their socks to stimulate the blood circulation!

Two great healthy vegetables for seasoning with:
Onion and Garlic

Known and cultivated all over the world, these plants are used in the preparation of many dishes. Back at the start of the Christian era Indian medical treatises described their diuretic effect and their beneficial influence on the digestive system. Onions were declared to be a medicine in France in 1837 and became components of a syrup or a wine prescribed for patients. The wine, which has a diuretic effect, is very easy to prepare.

Here is the recipe:

400 gr. onions
150 gr. honey
1 litre dry white wine (with low alcohol content)

Purée the onions in a blender, pass through a sieve and mix with the honey and the wine. Drink one cup or glass full daily.

Like garlic, onions work on the endocrine glands and improve the circulation of the blood. They protect from the consequences of excessive consumption of fat and prevent cholesterol from being deposited in the body. Garlic has been heralded for years as one of the greatest foods for a healthy heart - it has a beneficial effect on the circulation of blood and protects from high blood pressure. Plus it tastes great, too! Both garlic and onions are also said to support the elimination of worms from the intestines.

Herbal Teas and Infusions

Teas and infusions are prepared from dried plants that should be stored in airtight containers so that they do not lose their effect. Always label your containers with a date, because dried plants should be used up within one year of being harvested. Kept any longer than this and they lose their beneficial properties.

Preparing infusions

Pour hot water over the dried plant, or plants, and leave the liquid to draw in a covered vessel. It should draw for a sufficient time to allow certain substances to be dissolved in water (from 10 minutes to 1 hour, depending on whether the shoots, flowers or leaves are used). Camomile, mint, lime blossom and verbena can be prepared in this way.

Decoctions are made by continuously boiling plants for 10 to 30 minutes. Roots, shoots, seeds and fruits are prepared in this way.

Plants used for infusions and decoctions:

- **Caraway, anise or dill tea** will improve the digestion, is diuretic and helps with the elimination of wind. To better utilise the properties of these herbs their seeds should be ground before they draw.

- **Anise** supports the digestion and is anti-flatulent. Keep to the proportion of 4-5 flowers per litre of water and boil for 15 minutes.

- **Camomile** is a great calming herb, which also has a laxative and spasmolytic effect. (Not to be taken at the same time as homeopathic medicines!)

- **The pedicels (i.e., stalks) of cherries** are known for their diuretic effect.

- **Dog-rose fruits** contain a lot of vitamin C, which makes them a strong diuretic. It strengthens and prevents fatigue and also stimulates. Dog-rose tea makes a nice change to coffee or tea in a morning.

- **Verbena** is a laxative and supports the digestion. It also relieves pain.

The Tenth Commandment

The final secret: green tea

I now want to share with you '*my secret weapon*'.

If you carefully follow the first nine commandments you will gradually lose weight. It is the only way to lose weight and to keep your slim figure forever. Those of who you are impatient (as I used to be), will discover that impatience simply causes stress which makes losing weight more difficult. You have waited so long to find the method which works - the one I have just described to you - so don't go and undo all the good work by discarding these methods during the first week because of impatience.

However, I do understand how some of you need a definite push to start losing weight. If you have suffered from excess weight problems for years, you will have to wait for some weeks in order to regain the slim figure you have been dreaming of - it is not going to happen overnight, but it is SO WORTH WAITING FOR! It is precisely you people to whom I want to reveal my secret weapon to - this is the first time I have shared this information with anyone!

This natural and amazingly effective supplement has been extensively researched in a laboratory studying people's mood problems and consequential states of health - its benefits in weight loss were almost a by-product of this original research! I happened across the information while chatting to someone about healthy eating and was fascinated with all I heard. I had to find out for myself. Because it is a natural product I was happy to use it to supplement my already effective method - I didn't think things could get even better, but how wrong I was! You have to try this for yourself.

The secret weapon I discovered is '*green tea*', or more precisely drops containing green tea extract. This completely natural concentrate influences the metabolism by stimulating the elimination of fatty layers which have been stored for a long time - those very stubborn layers which are normally the hardest to shift.

All my reading and my investigations led me to understand that the active agents present in green tea work by almost "sucking in" the fat so it can then be eliminated. Whatever the technicalities are, believe me it really does work. The green tea drops helped my body to cleanse itself, which stopped it hoarding fat.

I highly recommend that you make these drops a part of your diet. The first nine commandments will ensure that you lose the superfluous kilos and will not regain them later. But add the green tea drops and you will get a kick-start. They will help you to shift the "old-established fat", which is normally the last and hardest part to lose. This fabulous double action will help you to become slimmer and healthier 'sooner'.

When I first noticed the positive results the drops were having on my body, I sought more information. I knew I had to share my discovery with people and wanted to be able to explain exactly how it works. I am certainly no scientist, but I found the following diagrams explanatory and helpful - I hope you do too.

I think that I have fully done what I set out to do with writing this little book. Now it's over to you. The decision is yours. You can do it. You can change your life just as I did. The you of the future is not only slimmer and more attractive, but so much healthier and more positive and happy, too. Just follow my Ten Commandments and you will never look back.

The way it works

Green Tea Capsules

poliphenol

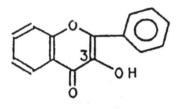

xantogen basis

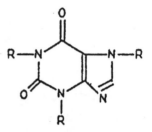

fights fat in the digestive system

reduces the layer of fatty tissue

Weight loss

Loss of superfluous centimetres

Effect 1

Effect 2

The effect: diagram 1

People subjected to the test lost weight, although they kept eating

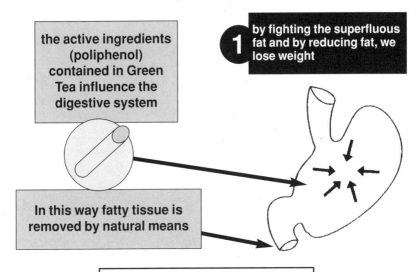

the active ingredients (poliphenol) contained in Green Tea influence the digestive system

1 by fighting the superfluous fat and by reducing fat, we lose weight

In this way fatty tissue is removed by natural means

The effect: diagram 2

How the xanto-gen bases work

Cross section of cellulite skin

BEFORE

Cross section of skin without cellulite

AFTER (loss of superfluous centimetres)

2 Eradication of fatty tissue

3 Extra centimetres lost thanks to the effect on the fats

Part 3:

The recipes

The recipes I suggest to you here will not only bring a great deal of variety to your daily meals; they will also ensure you get slimmer very quickly without losing any of your enjoyment of food. They are based on the French cuisine, because everyone knows that France is famous for its cuisine and its enjoyment of eating. (What's more, French women are famous for their good figures, despite their enjoyment of food... which just goes to prove my point, that you will never lose weight if you don't eat!) Apart from that, I personally love French cooking, especially the typical dishes of the South of France and the whole Mediterranean region.

Chicken soup

Provides around 1 litre of soup

1 kg lean chicken meat
1 small onion (approx. 50 gr.)
1 clove of garlic
1 1/2 litres of cold water
1 carrot, peeled
1 stick of celery
1 leek
1 sprig of thyme, dried
1 bay leaf
1 teaspoon of salt
12 black peppercorns

- Rinse the chicken meat under running water. Place in a large pot. Pour the cold water over and bring to the boil. Skim off the brown froth that will form, then add the vegetables, thyme, bay leaf, salt and pepper. Cover and leave to simmer over a low heat for two hours - or until approximately 1.2 litres of soup remain - and then strain.

- This delicate, aromatic broth can be used to prepare several meals. You can also freeze it in small portions to use as and when required.

Quark (Ricotta) cream cheese with herbs

Serves 6

250 gr. low-fat Quark or Ricotta (soft curd cheese)
60 ml olive oil
3 tablespoons white vinaigrette
3 tablespoons dry white wine
200 ml cold yoghurt
2 finely chopped shallots
6 sprigs of finely chopped parsley
Finely chopped leaves from 6 sprigs of chervil
1 small bunch of chives, finely chopped
Salt and freshly milled pepper

- In a dish mix together the Quark (or Ricotta) cheese with the olive oil, vinaigrette and white wine.

- Add the yoghurt to the mixture, and then add the chopped shallots, herbs and salt and pepper, stirring all the time. Cool in the refrigerator. Serve the Quark cream with a green salad or vegetable salad.

Fish Soup

Serves 6

1.5 kg various small white-fleshed fish
200 gr. green peppers
60 ml olive oil
1 onion, finely chopped
4 cloves of garlic, roughly chopped
1 leek (white part only), washed and dried
500 gr. ripe tomatoes, quartered
2 sprigs of dried dill
1 sprig of dried thyme
1 pinch of saffron
3 sprigs of parsley
1 bay leaf
2 litres of water
Salt to taste and freshly milled pepper

- Skin and gut the fish, then rinse and dry. Cut peppers into quarters, remove seeds then slice thinly.

- Heat the olive oil in a large pan. Add onion, garlic, pepper and leek. Cook over a low heat for 2 minutes, stirring. Add tomatoes, dill, thyme, saffron, parsley, bay leaf and the fish. Stir. Cover and simmer on a low heat for 10 minutes.

- Bring the water to the boil and pour into the pan. Add salt and pepper to taste. Cover and simmer over a low heat for 20 minutes.

Pumpkin soup

Serves 6

Two tablespoons butter
4 leeks (white part only), washed and sliced
750 gr. pumpkin, peeled and diced
750 ml. chicken soup
Salt and freshly milled pepper
250 ml. skimmed milk

- Melt half of the butter in a large pan. Fry the leeks, stirring all
  the time with a wooden spoon until they are soft and browned.
  Add the diced pumpkin, chicken soup and salt and pepper.
  Cook for 30 minutes or until the pumpkin is soft.

- Pour the mixture into the blender and purée. Reheat and add
  the rest of the butter and the milk. Stir well and remove from
  the heat. Pour into a tureen and serve immediately.

Carrot Soup

Serves 4

50 gr. butter
1 onion, finely chopped
2 leeks (white part only), washed and thinly sliced
2 litres of water
1 kg. young carrots, peeled and finely diced
Salt and freshly milled pepper
6 tablespoons (100 ml.) yoghurt

Melt half the butter in a large pan. Add the chopped onion and leeks and cook, stirring, for 3 minutes or until the vegetables are browned. Add the water and bring to the boil. Add the carrots and season with salt and pepper. Cover and cook over a low heat for 30 minutes or until the carrots are soft.

Pour the contents of the pan into the blender and purée for one minute at the highest speed until it becomes a creamy, homogenous mixture. Return to the pan and bring to the boil. Add the yoghurt and the rest of the butter. Pour into soup bowls and serve immediately.

Salade Niçoise

Serves 6

6 eggs
1 red pepper
1 lemon
1 clove of garlic
500 gr. firm tomatoes, cut into eighths
2 small to medium size onions (depending on your
preference), sliced
1 cucumber, sliced
2 stalks of celery, cut into thin strips (remove the strings)
1 tin (200 gr.) tuna in oil (fish sieved and chopped)
50 gr. black olives
12 large basil leaves
Salt to taste
6 tablespoons olive oil

Place eggs in a pan with cold water and bring slowly to the boil. Allow to boil for 10 minutes over a low heat. Cool under running water, peel and quarter.

Halve the peppers, remove the seeds and slice thinly.

Rub the peeled clove of garlic around the inside of a shallow dish. Place tomatoes, pepper, cucumber, onions and celery in the dish. Arrange the tuna, olives and hard-boiled eggs on the top. Sprinkle the salad with the chopped basil. Add salt and drizzle with olive oil to taste and serve immediately.

Stuffed Vegetables

Serves 6

3 eggplants (about 200 gr. each)
2 small zucchinis (about 100 gr. each)
6 ripe tomatoes (about 150 gr. each)
6 onions (about 100 gr. each)
Salt and freshly milled pepper
3 tablespoons olive oil
2 cloves garlic, finely chopped
500 gr. boneless veal (remove any fat and finely chop the meat)
1 bunch parsley (remove stalks and chop leaves)
50 gr. Parmesan cheese, finely grated
1 egg
2 small sprigs thyme

- Wash and dry the aubergines and courgettes, then cut length-ways and scoop out most of the centres so that only a 5 mm thick layer of flesh remains in the skins. Cut of the top quarter of each tomato and scoop out the flesh with a small spoon. Wash and peel the onions, cut off the tops and scoop out the middle layers. Season the insides of the vegetables with salt and pepper and brush with olive oil. Chop up all the removed vegetable flesh with a sharp knife.

- Heat 1 tablespoon of olive oil in a non-stick pan (26 cm. diameter). Add garlic, chopped vegetables and veal, and stir over a low heat for 5 minutes or until everything is lightly browned. Then place in a dish and allow to cool.

- Pre-heat the oven to 200°. Brush an ovenproof dish, large enough to hold all the vegetables, with olive oil.

- Add parsley, Parmesan cheese, thyme, salt and pepper to the cooled vegetables and stir well. Fill the vegetables with this mixture then place them in the ovenproof dish and brush with the remaining olive oil. Add about 60 ml. water to the dish. Bake in the oven for 45 minutes or until the vegetables are soft. Baste occasionally with the sauce produced during cooking and refill with water.

- When the vegetables are cooked, arrange them on a large platter, pour the sauce over them and serve.

White fish fillets

Serves 4

4 white fish fillets, about 200 gr. each
Salt and freshly milled pepper
100 gr. butter
1 tablespoon freshly squeezed lemon juice
2 tablespoons chopped parsley

Rinse and dry the fillets and then season with salt and pepper.

Melt half the butter in a non-stick pan and fry the fillets for 4 minutes on each side then place the fillets on 4 warmed plates. Add the remaining butter and the lemon juice to the fat in the pan. Melt the butter over a very low heat. Pour this sauce over the fillets and sprinkle with chopped parsley. Serve immediately with a tossed green salad, boiled new potatoes or rice, depending on your preference.

Marinated Mackerel

Serves 4

12 small mackerel, about 100 gr. each
Salt to taste
1 lemon, sliced
1 bay leaf, 1 sprig thyme, 6 sprigs parsley
500 ml. dry white wine
1 onion (approx. 100 gr.) sliced into rings
2 carrots, about 50 gr. each, peeled and cut into thin slices
2 tablespoons of white wine vinegar
2 cloves
1 teaspoon peppercorns
Pinch of red chili pepper (or more, depending on your preference)

- Gut the fish, rinse and dry them and then season with salt. Wash and dry the lemon and cut into thin slices. Tie the herbs together into a bunch.

- Pour the wine into a non-stick pan (26 cm. diameter). Add onion, carrots, lemon slices, vinegar, the bunch of herbs, cloves, salt, peppercorns and chili pepper. Bring to the boil and cook over a low heat for 10 minutes. Add the fish and continue cooking.

- Remove the fish and drain well. Continue cooking the liquor for at least 5 minutes until it is somewhat reduced. In a square earthenware dish place alternating layers of fish, onions, carrots and lemon slices. Strain the liquor, pour over the fish and cool. Cover the dish. Store for 12 hours in the refrigerator before serving.

Fish in aioli sauce

Serves 4

60 ml. olive oil
1 carrot, peeled and finely chopped
10 celery leaves, finely chopped
2 leeks, (white part only) finely chopped
Salt and freshly milled pepper
4 servings eel or cod, each approx. 250 gr. and 5 cm. thick.

For the sauce:
1 clove of garlic
1 teaspoon hot mustard
1 egg yolk
6 tablespoons of olive oil

Heat the olive oil in a frying pan. Add the chopped vegetables and cook over a low heat for about 10 minutes. Stir occasionally with a wooden spoon. Do not allow the vegetables to brown. Season fish with salt and pepper and place in the pan. Fry over a low heat for 10 minutes on each side.

While the fish is frying, prepare the aioli sauce: crush the garlic in a shallow dish, add mustard, egg yolk and salt and mix together. Leave to stand for one minute then slowly add olive oil and beat to a creamy consistency.

Place the cooked fish on a plate and keep warm. Remove the pan from the heat, add the aioli sauce and stir everything together, then pour the sauce over the fish and serve immediately.

Fried fish with dill

Serves 4

1 1/2 fish fillets (cod or hake)
Salt and freshly milled pepper
60 ml olive oil
10 sprigs dill

For the sauce:

1 clove of garlic
1 teaspoon of hot mustard
1 egg yolk
Salt and freshly milled pepper
6 tablespoons olive oil
1 teaspoon of white wine vinegar
2 finely chopped gherkins
1 tablespoon capers, drained and finely chopped
2 tablespoons of parsley, chopped
1 tablespoon of chives, chopped

- Rinse and dry the fish. Rub salt and pepper into both sides. Fill with some of the dill and then brush olive oil over the skin. Preheat the oven. Place the rest of the dill in an ovenproof dish and place in the oven. Place the fish on a baking tray and place this on top of the dill. Bake for 25 minutes, turning the fish over after 12 minutes.

- Meanwhile prepare the sauce. Crush the garlic in a shallow dish, add mustard, egg yolk, pepper and salt and mix together. Allow to stand for one minute, then slowly add the olive oil and mix to a creamy consistency. Add the white wine vinegar and continue stirring for 30 seconds, then add the chopped gherkins, capers, parsley and chives. Pour into a sauceboat. Serve the sauce separately.

Baked carp

Serves 4

1 carp, approximately 1.2 kg. in weight
500 gr. ripe tomatoes
60 ml olive oil
2 cloves garlic, finely chopped
1 tablespoon parsley, chopped
Salt and freshly milled pepper
1 lemon

Skin and gut the fish, then rinse and dry it.

Pre-heat the oven to 230°C. Dip the tomatoes into hot water for about 10 seconds, cool them under running water, peel, halve, remove seeds and chop.

Heat half the olive oil in a non-stick pan (26 cm. diameter). Add garlic and parsley and fry, stirring. Stir in the tomatoes and season with pepper and salt. Steam for about 5 minutes over a medium heat until the tomato juice has almost evaporated.

Place fish in a baking dish which should be big enough to hold the whole fish. Sprinkle with the rest of the olive oil and bake for 5 minutes.

Meanwhile wash and dry the lemon, then cut it into thin slices. Pour the tomato sauce over the fish, lay the lemon slices on top and bake for a further 30 minutes. Serve straight out of the baking dish.

Tuna fish à la Languedoc

Serves 6

1 fresh tuna fish fillet approximately 1.2 kg in weight and 2 cm. thick
Salt and freshly milled pepper
3 lemons
3 tablespoons of olive oil
10 cloves of garlic, peeled
500 ml. of dry white wine

Rinse and dry the tuna fish and then season with salt and pepper. Wash the lemons, cut two of them into thin slices, squeeze the juice from the third.

Heat the olive oil in a pan which is large enough to hold the whole fish fillet. Brown the fish lightly, this should take about 4 minutes on each side. Remove from the pan and keep warm. Fry the garlic cloves until they are brown, then place into the dish with the fish. Place wine and lemon juice in the pan and cook until reduced by half. Replace the tuna and the garlic cloves in the pan, cover and cook for 10 minutes, turning the fish after 5 minutes.

Place the fish and garlic in a shallow dish and keep warm. Heat the remaining mixture in the pan over a high heat until it becomes a creamy sauce. Pour this sauce over the fish and serve immediately.

Cod fillets with mangold and raisins

(A mangold is a form of beetroot.) If magnold's are not available in your area, you can substitute plain old beetroot or Swiss chard.

Serves 6

1 kg cod fillets
50 gr. raisins
500 gr. ripe tomatoes
500 gr. mangold
3 tablespoons olive oil
1 onion, finely chopped, approx. 100 gr.
1 cloves garlic, finely chopped
1 bay leaf
Salt and freshly milled pepper

- Rinse the fillets and cut them into 4 cm. square pieces. Rinse the raisins in hot water and drain. Cut the tomatoes into quarters and dice.

- Wash the mangold, drain and cut into 2 cm. strips. Place in a pan, add a little water, cover and cook for 4 minutes over a high heat and then strain.

- Heat the olive oil in a non-stick pan (26 cm. diameter). Add onion and garlic and fry for 2 minutes. Add the tomatoes and the bay leaf. Season with salt and pepper and cook gently over a very low heat for 15 minutes.

- Add the fish, mangold and raisins, cover and cook for a further 15 minutes over a low heat. Arrange in a shallow dish and serve while still hot.

Fish soup provençale

Serves 6-8

3 kg. various fish and mussels: cod, eel, perch, squid, sole, turbot, crab, lobster, crayfish, etc.
60 ml. olive oil
500 gr. coarsely chopped tomatoes
2 carrots, peeled and thinly sliced
1 leek, washed and thinly sliced
1 stick celery, thinly sliced
1 onion, approx. 100 gr. sliced into rings
1 sprig dried thyme
1 small sprig dried rosemary
1 sprig dried dill
1 bay leaf
1 strip dried orange peel
10 cloves of garlic, peeled
10 sprigs fresh parsley
1 pinch saffron
Salt and freshly milled pepper
500 ml. dry white wine

- Skin and gut fish, remove heads, keep to one side. Cut larger fish into pieces approximately 4 cm. in size, but leave smaller fish whole. Rinse and dry all fish. Cut lobster and crayfish lengthways into strips, remove heads and keep shells to one side. Wash and chop up the squid, keep bodies and tentacles on one side, rinse and dry.

- Heat the olive oil in a 6-litre pan. Add fish heads and shells and fry, stirring, for 5 minutes over a low heat. Add tomatoes, carrots, leek, celery and onion and cook, stirring, for a further 5 minutes or until the vegetables are brown. Add thyme, rosemary, dill, bay leaf, orange peel, garlic cloves, parsley, saffron, salt and pepper and whisk for one minute with an egg whisk. Add the wine and simmer for 45 minutes.

- Remove fish remnants, thyme, rosemary, dill, bay leaf, orange peel, garlic cloves and parsley. Purée the tomato mixture in a blender.

- Wipe out the pan and add the puréed mixture. Bring slowly to the boil over a low heat. Add the firmer fish first, then add the softer-fleshed fish, and bring each portion to the boil before adding the next portion. Lastly add the mussels, lobster and crayfish. Simmer for 10 minutes, and then with a slotted spoon remove the fish and mussels and place on a plate. Keep warm.

- Pour the soup into a tureen and serve. Serve the fish and mussels separately.

Chicken with tarragon vinegar

Serves 4 - 6

2 tomatoes, ripe, medium sized
1 chicken, approximately 1.5 kg. in weight, cut into eight pieces
Salt and freshly milled pepper
1 tablespoon vegetable oil
25 gr. butter
6 cloves of garlic, peeled
6 tablespoons of tarragon vinegar
150 ml. dry white wine
2 pinches of sugar
150 ml. yoghurt
1 tablespoon hot mustard

- Dip the tomatoes into boiling water for 10 seconds, rinse under running water, peel, halve, remove seeds and chop finely.

- Season chicken with salt and pepper. Heat the olive oil in a non-stick pan (26 cm. diameter); add the butter, chicken pieces and garlic cloves and fry for 10 minutes. Add the tarragon vinegar and simmer. Add the wine and tomatoes, season with salt, pepper and sugar. Cook for 45 minutes, stirring from time to time.

- In the meantime, mix the yoghurt with the mustard in a small dish. Remove the fried chicken pieces from the pan and keep warm. Sieve the sauce that has formed during the cooking and add the crushed cloves of garlic. Cook for 5 minutes over a high heat until the sauce has thickened. Add the mustard mixture and cook for a further two minutes over a high heat. Pour the sauce over the chicken pieces and serve immediately. Green vegetables or a vegetable salad would make an excellent accompaniment.

Chicken with garlic

To serve 5 - 6

1 chicken, approximately 1.75 kg. in weight
Salt
2 small sprigs of thyme
2 small sprigs of rosemary
1 sprigs of sage
2 young celery stalks with leaves
2 sprigs of parsley
8 of garlic
3 tablespoons of olive oil
Freshly milled pepper

Pre-heat the oven to 200° Centigrade. Rub salt all over the chicken and stuff with half the thyme, sage and celery, adding the parsley and 4 of the garlic cloves. Place the remaining herbs and celery in an oval, ovenproof dish large enough to hold the chicken. Add the olive oil, salt, pepper and the remaining cloves of garlic. Roll the chicken in the olive oil and place in the dish. Roast, covered, for 1 hour and 45 minutes. Place chicken on a platter. Pour off the sauce into a sauceboat. Serve the chicken with the sauce and either a green salad or a vegetable salad.

Chicken à la Basque

Serves 4 - 6

4 small green peppers
500 gr. ripe tomatoes
1 chicken approximately 1.5 kg. in weight, cut into eight pieces
Salt and freshly milled pepper
3 tablespoons of vegetable oil
2 onions, approx. 100 gr. each, finely chopped
3 cloves of garlic, finely chopped
1 slice of lean ham, finely diced
1 chili, finely chopped
150 ml. of dry white wine

- Cut the peppers in half lengthways, remove stalks and seeds. Dip the tomatoes into hot water for 10 seconds, cool under running water, peel, halve, remove seeds and chop finely.

- Season the chicken pieces with salt and pepper. Heat the oil in a non-stick pan (diameter 26 cm.) and sear the chicken on all sides. Remove the chicken pieces from the pan, add the onions and garlic and stir for one minute. Add the ham, peppers and chili and then fry, stirring; over a low heat for 5 minutes or until the vegetables are soft.

- Put the chicken pieces back into the pan, add the wine and cook over a high heat until the wine has evaporated. Add the tomatoes and season with salt and pepper. Cover and cook over a low heat for 45 minutes, stirring occasionally.

- Place the chicken in a shallow dish. Cook the sauce produced during cooking until it thickens then pour it over the chicken and serve immediately.

Chicken with herbs

Serves 6

150 gr. sorrel
150 gr. fresh spinach
150 gr. small leeks, white and green parts only
1 heart of lettuce
3 young celery stalks with leaves
4 sprigs of parsley
3 sprigs of tarragon
3 sprigs of chervil
2 sprigs of mint
1 chicken, approximately 2 kg. in weight, cut into 10 pieces
Salt and freshly milled pepper
25 gr. vegetable oil
200 ml. dry white wine
1 bunch chives, chopped
6 tablespoons low-fat yoghurt

- Wash spinach and sorrel leaves, drain and chop. Cut leeks, lettuce and celery into 1 cm. strips. Remove stalks from parsley, tarragon, chervil and mint and finely chop the leaves.

- Season the chicken with salt and pepper. Heat the oil in a round or oval 4-litre pan and brown the chicken pieces on all sides for 10 minutes. Remove the melted fat. Heat and stir the chicken pieces for one minute. Add the wine and bring to the boil. Add the vegetables and herbs and stir well. Cover and cook over a low heat, stirring occasionally.

- Stir in the yoghurt and cook for a further 30 minutes, stirring occasionally. When the chicken is cooked through, remove it and serve immediately with a green salad.

Pot roast beef à la Provençale

Serves 6

1.8 kg beef suitable for roasting, e.g. neck, entrecôte, rump, etc.
1 onion, approximately 100 gr.
2 cloves
1 sprig thyme
1 sprig sage
1 bay leaf
Leaves of 2 sticks of celery
2 strips of orange peel
750 ml. of red wine
3 tablespoons red wine vinegar
4 cloves garlic, peeled and quartered
3 tablespoons olive oil
250 gr. carrots, medium, peeled and cut into slices
Salt and freshly milled pepper
4 pinches freshly ground nutmeg

- Cut the meat into 5 centimetre cubes. Peel the onion and stud with cloves. Tie all the herbs into a bunch, place the meat in a large dish and pour over wine and red wine vinegar. Add the herbs, garlic and onion; cover the dish and leave to marinate in the refrigerator for 12 hours.

- Pre-heat the oven to 180°C.

- Heat the olive oil in a non-stick pan (28 cm. diameter). Add the carrots and fry over a high heat for 7-8 minutes until they are brown and caramelized. Season with salt, pepper and ground nutmeg; remove them from the pan with a slotted spoon and place to one side.

- Drain the meat and dry it. Lightly fry the meat in the same pan the carrots were in.

- Place the meat in a pot and cover with the carrots. Pour the wine marinade over it. Add the herbs, garlic and onion. Season with salt and pepper. Cover the pan with a sheet of waxed paper and place lid on top. Roast in the oven for approximately 5 hours.

- Remove the onion, garlic and bunch of herbs from the pan. If necessary, continue boiling the sauce for a few minutes over a high heat until it has thickened. Serve the meat with the carrots, sauce and either a green salad or a vegetable salad.

Spicy pot roast beef with vegetables

2 kg piece of beef (braising steak, neck, entrecôte, rump, etc.)
Salt and freshly milled pepper
1 teaspoon of your favourite powdered herbs
6 tablespoons of cognac or brandy
750 ml. of dry white wine
2 knuckles of veal, halved
100 gr. lean bacon rind
1 large onion
3 cloves
1 bay leaf
1 sprig thyme
6 sprigs parsley
3 tablespoons vegetable oil
25 gr. butter
1 carrot, peeled, sliced
3 garlic cloves, peeled
30 small pickled onions
10 baby carrots

- Dry the meat with kitchen paper. Mix salt, pepper and powered herbs and sprinkle over the meat. Place the meat in a deep, wide pot and pour over wine and cognac. The meat should be covered with the liquid. Cover and marinate in the refrigerator for 12 hours, turning the meat occasionally.

- Remove meat from the marinade and dry. Keep the wine mari-nade. Place the knuckles of veal and the bacon rind into a pan of boiling water and boil for 5 minutes. Remove, drain and cool under running water. Cut the bacon rind into large squares. Peel the large onion and stud with cloves. Tie herbs into a bunch.

- Heat 2 tablespoonfuls of oil and the butter in an oval ovenproof dish that is big enough to hold the meat. Sear the meat on all sides for 10 minutes. Add the knuckles of veal, the bacon rind, herbs, studded onion and whole garlic cloves. Pour in the wine marinade so that the meat is covered, adding more wine, water or beef stock as necessary. Season with salt and pepper, bring to the boil and cook for 5 hours over a very low heat.

- Meanwhile peel the small onions and carrots. Heat the remaining oil in a non-stick pan (28 cm diameter) and add the butter. When they have melted, add the onions and carrots and fry them, stirring gently, until they are caramelized. Then add the beef stock and simmer the vegetables for 20 minutes over a low heat until they are soft.

- When the meat has cooked for 5 hours, remove the pot from the heat. Remove the meat from the veal knuckle and dice it and the bacon rind. Place the meat on a platter. Garnish with veal, bacon rind, glazed onions and carrots. Keep warm.

- Sieve the aromatic, thick sauce that will have formed during cooking into a sauceboat. Put one slice of beef, a few cubes of veal, bacon rind the glazed vegetables on a plate, pour the sauce over and serve with either a green salad or a vegetable salad.

Pasta and vegetables

Serves 6

1 bay leaf
1 sprig of thyme
1 sprig of rosemary
6 sprigs of parsley
500 gr. ripe tomatoes
60 ml. of olive oil
250 gr. Onions, sliced into thin rings
6 garlic cloves, finely chopped
250 ml. dry white wine
Salt and freshly milled pepper
4 pinches of freshly ground nutmeg

Serve with
375 gr. fresh pasta

- Tie all the herbs into a bunch. Dip the tomatoes into boiling water for 10 seconds, cool under running water, peel, halve, remove seeds and chop roughly.

- Heat the olive oil in a 4-litre pot, add the onions and garlic and fry for two minutes, stirring continuously with a wooden spoon. Add the tomatoes and herbs. Add the wine and stir everything well. Season with salt, pepper and nutmeg, bring to the boil and cook, covered, for 15 minutes.

- To prepare the pasta: place in boiling water and boil until soft. Drain and arrange in a shallow dish. Pour over the sauce and mix well. Season with pepper and serve immediately with either a green salad or a vegetable salad.

Pepper steak

Serves 2

1 piece loin of beef, approximately 400 gr. in weight and around 3 cm thick
Salt
1 tablespoon crushed peppercorns
60 gr. of butter
2 tablespoons cognac
3 tablespoons low-fat yoghurt

- Prepare the meat: cut it into two steaks of equal sizes, dry and season with salt. Place the crushed peppercorns on a plate and roll the steaks in them.

- Melt half the butter in a non-stick pan (26 cm. diameter). Fry the steaks over a high heat for 2-3 minutes, as preferred. Add the cognac and light. When the flames have subsided, remove the steaks from the pan and place on plates. Keep warm.

- Wipe the pan and add the yoghurt. Cook over a high heat for one minute, then add the rest of the butter.

• Beef with spring vegetables

Serves 6

1.6 kg. beef
Salt and freshly milled pepper
200 gr. ripe tomatoes
1 bay leaf
1 sprig thyme
6 sprigs parsley
1 tablespoon vegetable oil
50 gr. butter
500 ml. chicken stock
2 garlic cloves, halved
500 gr. fresh peas
500 gr. small baby carrots
500 gr. baby kohlrabi
18 spring onions
200 gr. green beans
1 teaspoonful sugar
1 tablespoon chervil, chopped

Cut the meat into 5 cm. Cubes and season with salt and pepper. Dip the tomatoes into boiling water for 10 seconds, peel them, halve them, remove seeds and chop finely. Add all the herbs.

Heat the oil in an ovenproof 4-litre pot, add half the butter and the pieces of meat and brown lightly on all sides. Add tomatoes, stock, herbs and garlic to the pot, cover and cook over a low heat for one hour.

Meanwhile prepare the vegetables: pod the peas, peel the carrots and the kohlrabi, peel and cut the green off the spring onions, string the beans if necessary. Cook all the vegetables together in hot water for five minutes, drain.

Melt the rest of the butter in a non-stick pan (28 cm. diameter). Add the carrots, kohlrabi and onions and cook over a low heat for 5 minutes, stirring, until they are lightly browned. Add the beans and peas, sprinkle with sugar, salt and pepper. Cook for 2 minutes. Add 200 ml. chicken stock and cook for 15 minutes over a low heat.

When the meat has been cooking for an hour, add the vegetables to the ovenproof pot and warm over a low heat for five minutes. Remove the meat and vegetables with a slotted spoon and place in a deep dish. Keep warm. Cook the sauce that has formed during cooking until it thickens, then remove the garlic and herbs. Stir in the chervil. Pour the sauce over the meat and vegetables and serve immediately.

Pour this sauce over the steaks and serve immediately.

Pork with Brussels sprouts

Serves 4

1 fillet of pork
Salt and freshly milled pepper
1 tablespoon vegetable oil
60 gr. butter
500 gr. Brussels sprouts
200 ml water

- Tie the meat together with cooking twine. Season with salt and pepper. Heat the oil in an oval pot. Add half the butter and fry the meat on all sides. Remove from the pot. Place Brussels sprouts into the pot and fry for 4-5 minutes, stirring continuously. Put the meat back into the pot, add the water, bring to the boil, cover and simmer for 1 hour, turning the meat and sprouts occasionally.

- When the meat is cooked, place in a dish with the sprouts and serve immediately.

Chicken fillets with mushrooms

Serves 8

60 gr. dried mushrooms
8 chicken fillets
1 white onion
250 gr. tomatoes
1 tablespoon olive oil
1 cup of dry white wine
1/3 cup of parsley, finely chopped
3 tablespoons basil

- Pour a little cold water over the mushrooms and leave them to soak while you are preparing the other ingredients. Wash the chicken fillets. Peel and chop the onion. Wash the tomatoes and cut into strips.

- Heat the olive oil in a pan, add the onions and allow them to glaze. Fry the fillets on both sides. Add the wine, parsley, basil and tomatoes.

- Drain the mushrooms and slice them thinly.

- Add the mushrooms to the other ingredients in the pot, cover and warm through for 10 minutes over a low heat. Serve with a green salad.

Aubergine, pepper and pasta salad

450 gr. pasta
450 gr. aubergines
3 tablespoons olive oil
1 cup wine vinegar
2 medium green peppers
3 large red peppers
1/3 cup parsley, finely chopped
4 small tomatoes
3 garlic cloves
1 coffee spoon cayenne pepper

- In a large pot bring the water to the boil. Add salt and pasta. Stir occasionally while cooking. Drain, refresh with cold water and drain again.

- Pre-heat the oven.

- Wash the aubergines, cut off both ends. Cut in half lengthways, brush with olive oil on one side and place on aluminium foil. Pour a spoonful of wine vinegar over each half and place in the oven.

- Wash, de-seed and quarter the peppers, place them skin side up next to the halved aubergines and roast them. Remove from the oven and leave to cool. Peel and rinse the quarter peppers and chop them into small pieces. Place in a large dish.

- Peel the aubergines, mince them and mix with the peppers. Add parsley.

- Wash the tomatoes, remove the seeds and the ends of the stalks, slice them and place them in the dish.

- Add the rest of the olive oil and the wine vinegar. Crush the garlic clove and add it. Season with cayenne pepper. Add the pasta and stir well.

Italian minestrone soup

Serves 10

2 tablespoons crushed garlic cloves
2 small courgettes, cut into small cubes
1 cup spinach, chopped
1 cup tomatoes, finely chopped
1 cup carrots, cut into small cubes
1 cup onions, finely chopped
1 cup celery, finely chopped
1 cup parsley, finely chopped
350 ml tomato juice
2 tablespoons top quality olive oil
1 cup small pasta shapes

Heat the olive oil in a large pot and fry each vegetable in turn.

Place all the ingredients (except the pasta shapes) in the pot and heat for 20 minutes. If necessary, add more water. Then add the pasta shapes and boil for a further 15 minutes.